Political Argument

A Guide to Research, Writing, and Debating

Marc Ménard

OXFORD
UNIVERSITY PRESS

OXFORD
UNIVERSITY PRESS

Oxford University Press is a department of the University of Oxford.
It furthers the University's objective of excellence in research, scholarship,
and education by publishing worldwide. Oxford is a registered trade mark of
Oxford University Press in the UK and in certain other countries.

Published in Canada by
Oxford University Press
8 Sampson Mews, Suite 204,
Don Mills, Ontario M3C 0H5 Canada

www.oupcanada.com

Library and Archives Canada Cataloguing in Publication
Ménard, Marc, 1956-, author
Political argument : a guide to research, writing, and debating
/ Marc Menard.

Includes bibliographical references and index.
ISBN 978-0-19-901874-1 (paperback)

1. Political science--Philosophy--Textbooks. 2. Political science--
Research--Textbooks. 3. English language--Rhetoric--Textbooks.
4. Academic writing--Textbooks. I. Title.

JA71.M38 2015   320.01   C2015-904234-8

Cover image: © iStock/traffic_analyzer

Oxford University Press is committed to our environment.
This book is printed on Forest Stewardship Council® certified paper
and comes from responsible sources.

Printed and bound in Canada
1 2 3 4 — 19 18 17 16

Contents

Preface

This book will serve the reader in two ways: first, it is a how-to guide to researching, writing, and debating in politics; and second, it offers reasons why argumentation is a matter of quality of life. The book began as a small how-to social sciences manual to be shared with students and colleagues. But Oxford University Press asked me to turn it into a book, and since I believe that people are more likely to dedicate themselves to learning when they understand the need, I began to explore what makes argumentation essential to our survival. In fact, I have come to believe that the act of arguing itself exercises the plasticity of the mind that has made our species, *Homo sapiens*, masters of survival.[1] We do things better when we have had a good argument about it. This is as true in marriage or in the classroom as it is in Parliament.

The imperative to offer the reader a deeper understanding also comes from a series of socio-political trends that worry me as a parent, a teacher, and a citizen. These trends seemed to be connected to a general decline in our democracy and in the current ability of politicians and citizens both to make and to recognize a good argument.

The first of these trends is that being a "good citizen" is falling out of fashion. According to a survey by Samara Canada, an organization dedicated to connecting citizens to politics, Canadians are less likely to participate in politics than ever before. Today's citizens may follow the law, pay their taxes, and give to charities, but fewer are participating in the act of voting. Fifty years ago, the rate of voter participation in elections was 80 per cent. Today, it is around 60 per cent in federal elections and much lower at the other levels of government. Plus political volunteerism is on the decline with fewer than 10 per cent of Canadians volunteering during elections, donating to political parties, or belonging to a political party.[2] This book offers an explanation of why citizen participation matters and what it might look like.

Another worrisome trend is the war that is being waged in our schools and in the media against the value of the humanities and the liberal arts to an education. In one of many recent articles of its kind, Alex

Preston of *The Guardian* wrote that educational programs "are under attack by an austerity-obsessed governments looking to maintain the excellence of our institutions at a fraction of the cost."[3] Indeed, that view may be symptomatic of another trend in modern capitalist societies: we are becoming market societies where everything is for sale and nothing is done unless it generates a profit. Consequently, unless a course or program is directly connected to vocational outcomes and suitable salaries, it is eliminated. Our educational institutions are no longer educating citizens; rather, they exist to provide a steady stream of trained workers to industry. And so, I thought it important to show how liberal arts courses such as those in political science helps keep life civilized and helps citizens, socially, economically and politically.

Yet another trend is a general feeling that seems to be creeping into the media and popular discourse that our democracy is broken. This malaise was exemplified by a recent *CBC Asks* debate on the question "Is Politics Broken?"[4]

This debate highlighted the fact that politics is messy, especially in a democracy. As I pointed out in *Canadian Democracy: A Concise Introduction*, teaching and following the unfolding of political events in the day-to-day life of a democracy is not for the faint of heart. But without educated citizens, democracies begin to unravel, and sometimes, even the proposed cures for social, political and economic ills may be worse than the disease. We need a broad and intelligent debate in Canadian society about how to improve our political system without causing changes that make it difficult for us to manage conflict power.

I teach politics in what is arguably one of the most culturally diverse educational institutions on the planet, where I am reminded daily of two incontrovertible truths: the first is that each one of us is different, right down to our DNA; and the second is that approaches both to teaching and to politics that do not account for diversity are unlikely to succeed. Democratic approaches seem to work best because they provide opportunities for listening, learning, offering opinions, and changing one's mind. When democratic approaches are not used, the potential for conflicts to escalate beyond words increases. This book offers an answer to that danger by showing the reader how to apply the principles of political science to argumentation.

Acknowledgements

My family and friends will tell you that I don't win nearly as many arguments as I would like, and that is a very good thing. I am a better person for it.

A loving thank you to my wife Liz and my daughters Laura, Catherine, and Carolyn.

I would like to thank my friends and colleagues at Seneca College, including Claire Moane, chair of the School of English and Liberal Studies, and professors Mark Rubinstein and Ken Sproul and especially Peter Macdonald, who helped with the online Social Sciences Guide. Peter was also a sounding board for some of the ideas in this book.

A world without librarians would be a dreary place. I would like to thank Joanna Blair and all the librarians at Seneca Libraries for their assistance.

Many thanks to Katherine Skene, acquisitions editor at Oxford University Press, who immediately saw that a draft originally written as an appendix to *Canadian Democracy: A Concise Introduction* would make a good textbook. *Political Argument* would not be possible without the help of OUP developmental editors, Mark Thompson and Meg Patterson, and my copy editor, Freya Godard.

I am grateful for teachers like my epistemology professor Patrick Maynard of the University of Western and my Ottawa University thesis advisor, Professor Paul Dussault.

Finally, I would like to acknowledge the contributions made by public broadcasters in Canada and the United States, including the Canadian Broadcasting Corporation (CBC), TV Ontario (TVO), and the Public Broadcasting System (PBS) for elevating the public discourse above partisan and private interests. Like a good friend, public broadcasters tell us want we need to hear, not simply what we want to hear.

To argue well is to live well.

Introduction
Valuing the Political Argument

Turn on to politics or politics will turn on you.

Ralph Nader, 2004 Presidential Campaign Slogan

Each of us can point to personal examples of where a lack of proper information, an incomplete analysis, or a lack of clarity has had undesirable consequences. Consequences can range from mild, such as embarrassment or poor grades, to more serious, such as financial loss and even injury and death. Better outcomes for individuals and society are more likely when there is proper research, clear communication, and effective argumentation. The idea that a world with good arguments is better than a world without occurs to me every day as I read the newspaper, teach a class, or deal with my colleagues or my employer. This guide to researching writing and debating in political science is grounded in the belief that argumentation is a key ingredient in civil society and that education in the art of the argument can improve our quality of life. My purpose in this guide is to show that to argue well is to live well.

For me, one particular example of the importance of argumentation to civil society stands out. I recall the very moment that I heard the phrase "Turn on to politics or politics will turn on you." It was an afternoon in the fall of 2004, and my head was still reeling from having seen the movie *Hotel Rwanda*, which depicts the Rwandan genocide and the massacre of 800,000 Tutsis by members of the Hutu majority and with the full support of much of the country's political elite. Moments after watching the movie, I was listening to CBC Radio in my car and heard an interview the US independent presidential candidate and political activist, Ralph Nader. His campaign slogan, "Turn on to politics or politics will turn on you" resonated with me at that moment; politics had indeed "turned" on a large portion of the Rwandan people. Nader's slogan was an invitation to the American electorate to avoid political calamity by voting for him instead of the incumbent, George Bush, or the Democratic Party nominee, John Kerry, and to avoid possibly ruinous political decisions such as declaring war on Iraq and Afghanistan. The Rwandan genocide, like the Holocaust and the killing fields of Cambodia, defy belief and rational explanation. Nader's slogan suggested that citizens could somehow avoid political calamity by turning on to politics. This led me to wonder about the fragility of our civilization and what makes civilization possible. Maybe the French philosopher and lawyer Joseph de Maistre was correct when he said after the French Revolution, "Every country has the government it deserves." But how could the citizens of those countries allow their governments to act in such uncivilized ways? What pushes citizens to commit brutal acts of violence against one another? And finally, how can humans maintain civilization and avoid these calamities?

Ralph Nader's slogan seemed to offer a solution: get the citizens "turned on" to politics. Nader's solution is reminiscent of Thomas Hobbes's concept of popular sovereignty, namely, that the "people" hold the key to all government action. The people's support, tacit or otherwise, is essential for the state to exist or to act. In other words, the people can prevent governments from acting in ways that are contrary to the public good.

But what do we mean by "turned on"? What would it look like? And just how "turned on" should a citizen be? Surely, the French citizens were turned on to politics when they took part in the Reign of Terror during the French Revolution, as were the Brown Shirts and Hitler Youth when they committed their atrocities against the Jews and other minorities after the Nazis took control of the German government in 1933. On the other hand, we see examples of positive and civilized civic engagement whenever there is a democratic election and a peaceful change of government or an organized humanitarian response to a natural disaster. It seemed to me that Mr Nader's ideas on civic engagement warranted further exploration and explanation.

For me, two truths have emerged from my years of observing, studying, and teaching politics; the first is that *insecurity, and not money, is the root of all evil*; the second truth is that the most effective remedy against insecurity is argumentation, tempered with critical thinking.

For the proof of those truths we need only speak to the refugees, the landed immigrants, and the new Canadians. Why come to a country like Canada or the United States? What makes it preferable to trade the country one is familiar with for one with different weather, laws, social mores, language, economy, and so on? Could it be that the insecurity of moving to a new country is preferable to the economic or political insecurity of the country of origin? It would appear that the answer is "yes." The attraction for most new Canadians comes from the fact that some countries, like Canada, have been able to create a fertile and secure ground in which civilization can flourish—for the moment at least. One could argue that at this moment in history, liberal democracies like Canada, the United States, and European states have systems of liberty and governance that come from the incorporating of critical-thinking principles and practices into the daily management of their social, economic, and political institutions. The citizens of these countries have been practising these principles and skills in ways that improve their quality of life. In these political systems, argumentation is seen as a way of improving society. The skills and practices necessary for critical reasoning and argumentation are encouraged in their educational system, social relationships, and public institutions. To argue well is to live well.

Instinct and Reason

Refugees and landed immigrants tell us stories not only of economic hardship but also of war and threats of violence. They note that the threats of violence come from those who feel insecure themselves and believe that they are threatened or might be abused in some way. Critical-thinking skills are sometimes purposely disengaged from the political institutions that manage a society. In the extreme, the *idea* takes hold in the public's mind that there is some source of insecurity, some economic, political, physical, or psychological force, whether internal or external, that must be fought or destroyed. There may not be a factual basis for these feelings, but the mere belief in the *idea* of a threat is sufficient for people to act in ways that are irrational and destructive to others of even to themselves. Thomas Hobbes likened the descent of civilization to a state of war and the return to the natural impulses that might help us survive in nature, where there is no rule of law:

> To this war of every man against every man, this also is consequent: that nothing can be unjust. The notions of right and wrong, justice and injustice, have there no place. Where there is no common power, there is no law; where no law, no injustice. Force and fraud are in war the cardinal virtues.[1]

Why does insecurity have such a powerful influence on human behaviour? And why is it a constant threat to civilization? The simple reason is that humans are hard-wired to act *intuitively* and *instinctively* to apparent threats, and irrationality trumps rationality. Fear elicits an immediate response in people, whereas critical thinking, researching, debating, and the weighing of options all take time, energy, and resources such as research data, scientific instruments, and money to pay for people's time. In fact, **intuition** is defined in the *Canadian Oxford Dictionary* as the *power of understanding situations or people's feelings immediately, without the need for conscious reasoning or study*. Not only is intuition essential to our survival, particularly when we have no time to think, but it also provides us with fundamental and immediate information that we use in all aspects of our daily lives.

To illustrate that point, we can look at the very common act of perceiving colours. When we look at the colour *green*, for example, we immediately *understand* that we are seeing *green* without an intervening rational thought process. We **understand** *green* in the sense of having "*a sympathetic awareness of the character or the nature of something*,"[2] but not in the sense of understanding something through our intellect and our ability to reason. Similarly, when we perceive a threat, and have no time to indulge in critical reasoning, such as "I perceive that I am being stalked by a polar bear," our instincts (that is, our sympathetic response system) kick in: survival becomes the prime objective, and research, writing, and debating are quickly forgotten. Therefore, we run.

The strategy of running away may or may not be successful, since polar bears can outrun humans. However, when we are not pressed for time, we have the capacity to come up with a reasoned response to that polar bear threat. This reminds me of the Inuit story of a boy who allows a polar bear to hunt him, and he leaves a trail of frozen whale blubber loaded with flexible bone shards that eventually kill the bear once it has eaten them. That is where critical thinking comes into play as we consider which weapons or strategies we can use to survive.

Another fact to emerge from looking at the calamities that result from human insecurity is that the sympathetic responses are much easier to harness when there is, or appears to be, a threat, and easier for political leaders to use to affect social outcomes. Our sympathetic responses, also known as fight-or-flight responses, tend to engage our nervous system and other mechanisms quickly without much conscious thought. On the other hand, applying critical-thinking and argumentation skills and the development of reasoned strategies and responses to problems or threats time, practice and a certain amount of developed intelligence. It turns out that education really does matter.

In cases where rational argumentation is replaced by irrational argumentation, we see a tendency to cast aside scientific research and critical thinking; these complex and time-consuming responses are sacrificed on the altar of the so-called "just cause." Rational argumentation, then, is no longer seen by the citizens and their government as a tool that can serve society. Weak and faulty arguments are made to create anger and fear and to mobilize the population. And what replaces constructive criticism and rational arguments is a campaign of propaganda and suppression by the organs of the state.

Propaganda is an organized program of publicity, selected information, or even distortions of the truth used to propagate a doctrine or practice or policy; it replaces scientific reasoning, critical thinking, civilized debate, and reasonable compromise. **Suppression**, in the political sense, is an act by the organs of the state to manipulate the truth and discourage open discussion. Those persons and organizations whose job it is to offer reasoned and balanced criticism of government policy, such as academics, intellectuals, opposition parties, government watchdogs, and the media are marginalized, imprisoned, or even killed. Propaganda and suppression have one purpose: to prevent political dissent by controlling ideas. Political messages are crafted to manipulate people's actions and behaviour; critical thinking is stifled; and uncritical thinking is not only encouraged, but valued. And from these ideas come actions, like the ones seen in 1980s Rwanda, the rise of the fascism in 1930s Europe, and Senator Joe McCarthy's "red scare" in 1950s America, that may not always serve the best interests of society.

One worrisome trend that seems to be enveloping American and Canadian politics is the decline in rational discussions about topics of social and political importance. It seems that arguments based on facts are no longer held in high regard and that arguments which appeal to instinct and emotion are seen by the media and the public as equal to or better than solid scientific research and well-reasoned arguments. Most recently in Canadian politics, we have seen a growing trend by the government to alter and dismantle some of the elements that make democracy and civil society function. Some examples are the cancelling of the long-form census, the muzzling of Canadian bureaucrats and scientists, the attacks against government watchdogs, and the cutbacks to public information institutions such as the CBC.

In his book *Enlightenment 2.0: Restoring Sanity to Our Politics, Our Economy, Our Lives*, the University of Toronto philosophy professor Joseph Heath describes the growing divide between those who believe in reasoned argument and those who believe that if something feels true, it must be true. Facts and science no longer seem to matter in the least.

The big tent of American politics has always sheltered its share of crazies, particularly gun nuts and religious conservatives, but in recent years they have been joined by the anti-tax Tea Party movement, the birthers (who deny that Obama was born in the United States), the truthers (who believe that the collapse of the World Trade Center towers was an inside job), and a dog's breakfast of antiscience denialists who believe in neither evolution nor global warming and who are highly suspicious of much else besides. There came a point, however, when the sideshow began to take over centre stage. Americans woke up to find that their political system was increasingly divided, not between right and left, but between crazy and non-crazy. And what's more, the crazies seemed to be gaining the upper hand.[3]

To sum up Heath's argument, there seems to be a battle between rationalists and irrationalists. Heath says that according to modern cognitive science the human mind is composed of different and "partially redundant and conflicting" parts:

> System 1 is the *intuitive, heuristic system*, which is rapid, unconscious and automatic. This system is rapid, computationally powerful, associative, and pragmatic. It takes little effort, does not require the resources of a working memory, and is not connected to individual differences in intelligence.
>
> System 2 is the *rational, analytic system* linked with language and reflective consciousness. It is high effort, slow and sequential. This system is linked to working memory ad intelligence, is capable of abstract hypothetical thinking, and is responsive to instructions and stated intentions.[4]

And so the reason that the "irrationalists" seem to be winning the argument is that it is so much easier and faster to appeal to emotional and irrational arguments than it is to argue scientifically and rationally. Heath says that for humans, thinking rationally is unnatural; our natural impulse is to use intuition-based thinking and retaliatory thinking. It turns out that reasoning, solving problems, and overcoming biases is hard work and requires discipline and training. For "reason" to do good work for society, it needs "social scaffolding"—a system of social, economic, and political support—because humans are far more rational when they collaborate and build argumentation into their social mores and political institutions.[5] There needs to be an appreciation of the benefit of argumentation for the public. Instead, both in Canada and the United States, some politicians have accused members of the media of having a "liberal" bias simply for publicizing facts. In a sense, these politicians are saying that the facts themselves have a liberal bias, which is irrational because facts do not have a bias: they simply *are*. In so doing, the political leaders are attempting to exploit certain elements of our irrationality and create an environment that is increasingly hostile to rationality. Irrationality, if the public are fearful and unsophisticated or uneducated, is much easier for politicians to exploit than rationality.

> As human beings, we depend heavily on our environment in order to reason correctly, but our environment is constantly evolving, undergoing process of reverse adaptation that favors cultural artifacts that exploit our irrationality. And so we have to work harder and harder as time goes by, because our intuitive problem-solving strategies become increasingly inept. And because the cognitive resources needed to override our misfiring heuristics are intrinsically scarce, we find ourselves falling further and further behind.[6]

In his book *The Lesser Evil: Political Ethics in an Age of Terror*, Michael Ignatieff writes about the freedom to choose what we believe in a liberal democracy. He argues that to compel anyone to believe is to violate one of the basic tenets of a liberal democracy, and so, he says we are "stuck" with the only instrument of cohesion we have left: persuasion. Ignatieff writes about the power of good arguments:

> It is a condition of our freedom that we cannot compel anyone to believe in the premises of a liberal democracy. Either those premises freely convince others or they are useless. They cannot be imposed, and we violate everything we stand for if we coerce those who do not believe what we do. In any event, we cannot pre-emptively detain all the discontent from our midst.
>
> So we are stuck, as we should be, with persuasion, with the duty, now more urgent than at any time in our history, to persuade each and every person who lives among us, whether as citizen or visitor, of two perfectly plain propositions: that we

are committed to respect their dignity, and if they fail to respect ours, we will defend ourselves. The threat of terror, the possibility of a terrorist outcome if we fail to convince one of these super empowered loners, makes the burden of justification that falls upon every citizen as a condition of membership in a liberal society heavier than it has even been. We must be able to defend ourselves—with force of arms, but even more with force of argument. For arms without argument are used in vain. Since I believe in the arguments, since I believe that human beings are unique in their capacity to be persuaded, changed, even redeemed by good ones, I do not doubt that we will prevail.[7]

It seems almost too obvious to say that in order for liberal democracies to work, we need engaged citizens who have the capacity to reason, argue, and persuade—and be persuaded—for the greater good. But if those capabilities are not present, have not been nurtured, or have been dismantled by the very leaders who were entrusted with their care, we have a serious problem. The very thing that makes liberal democracies strong, which is the freedom to choose what we believe in and to persuade others, may also be its Achilles heel because without the proper safeguards that education provides, this freedom also leaves the public vulnerable to deception and manipulation. If indeed humans have the capacity to persuade and to be persuaded, how does a society encourage those capabilities for the greater good?

Developing Critical Thinkers

Some citizens may be more open to the ideas in a well-reasoned argument and less likely to be deceived by emotional and irrational arguments and by those who want to control ideas for political advantage. We call these individuals *critical thinkers*. When confronted with an argument, critical thinkers will ask themselves: What is it that I am being asked to accept? What is the basis of the argument? Is the evidence used to support the argument true and valid?

The uncritical thinker is likely to accept the premises being offered on faith or for its emotional appeal, and will not seek out evidence that challenges the basis of an idea or course of action. According to R. Paul and L. Elder, some argumentation may be the product of what they call "egocentric thinking." Egocentric thinkers tend not to question the basis of arguments and tend not to think of the rights of others; they tend not to recognize the self-serving perspective of their points of view. Paul and Elder list five types of egocentric thinking:

Innate egocentrism: "It's true because I believe it."
What I believe is true even though I have never questioned my beliefs.

Innate sociocentrism: "It's true because we believe it."
Beliefs in the group I belong to are true even though they are never questioned.

Innate wish fulfillment: "It's true because I want to believe it."
Does not require a change in my thinking and belief in what "feels good."

Innate self-vaccination: "It's true because I have always believed it."
Strong desire to maintain beliefs that have been long held.

Innate selfishness: "It's true because it is in my selfish interest to believe it."
Beliefs that justify getting more power, money, or personal advantage even though there's no evidence to support such beliefs.[8]

According to Paul and Elder, the good news is that there is a cure for uncritical thinking; egocentric thinkers can become aware of the self-serving nature of their ideas and actions with education and with training. The uncritical thinker can learn to construct a rational argument, but also, and more importantly, distinguish a bad argument from a good one. We call that "critical thinking."

The Case for Controlled Conflict

There is a misconception in this era of "safety first" that our society should try to eliminate all forms of stress and risk, that all "conflict is bad" and arguments are to be avoided at all costs. On occasion the media report complaints by schoolteachers who are so appalled at the behaviour of our members of Parliament during question period in the House of Commons that they suggest removing question period from their tours of our nation's capital. Perhaps they are afraid that their students will get the idea that the MPs' behaviour would be appropriate in the classroom. MPs themselves, such as the Conservative MP Michael Chong, have recognized the decline in rational debate and civility in the House of Commons and have tried to do something about it.[9]

A quick look at the historical record will show that question period has hardly ever been a place of decorum and polite exchanges. Rather our parliamentary system of government (modelled after the Westminster, or British, parliamentary system of government) is designed to allow a competition of interests for the sake of the common good. And question period is a feature of that system for holding the government to account in an open and democratic way. Who said that democracy had to be pretty to look at? Our system of government may not be a paragon of politeness, but it has some 800 years of tradition and of evolution; and it works!

One could also say that marriage has the same built-in design elements as a parliament. Marriage has stood the test of time not only for reproductive purposes but also because when arguing between spouses is not abusive, when there is a frank exchange of views, and when the other person's point of view is taken into account, there tends to be compromise and better outcomes for the couple, the family and in turn for society. If marriage did not provide benefits beyond reproduction, why would couples choose to live together at all?

And in friendship or professional relationships, who needs friends or colleagues that always tell you what you want to hear? As Christopher Hitchens remarked in *Letters to a Young Contrarian*, "Allow a friend to believe in a bogus prospectus or a false promise and you cease, after a while, to be a friend at all."

Conflict then, under the proper conditions and with suitable guidelines or supervision, can be a force for good. In fact, the political institutions, educational systems, and social conventions of our liberal democracies have evolved to a point where we have the capacity to harness the energy that comes from conflict. We do this by managing arguments—tempering them with the elements of critical thinking—in order to control the conflict and allow the energy of the conflict to be harnessed for the benefit of the **commonwealth**, that is, "a community of people viewed as a political entity in which everyone has an interest." In short, our political institutions are designed to allow citizens and competing interests to argue and resolve conflict in safe and peaceful environments. In the long run, we benefit from this interaction. Managing conflict is how we keep our society civilized and prosperous. To examine this claim in more detail and why we tend to do better with rational argumentation than without it, we need to look at the nature of argumentation.

Arguments: What Are They? And Where Do We Find Them?

A good place to start any argument is with a definition.

In its most basic form, an **argument** is *an exchange of views.* But why do all humans engage in argumentation? That is likely because **argumentation** is *methodical reasoning designed to prove, make clear, or advance a point of view.* Arguments are the precursor to making decisions. For better or worse, the end product of argumentation is a decision that is intended to advance personal or social gain. Argumentation is part of **critical thinking**, which is *the systematic evaluation or formulation of belief statements by rational standards.*[10] The best arguments make us believe in the rational and what is *reasonably,* but not absolutely, possible. Plato called this "justified true belief."

Arguments, no matter what form or shape, good or bad, take place at every level of society, in every social relationship, and even between societies. At its core, *arguing is a political act* because it seeks to change the actions and behaviour of others and sets up power relations between actors. And arguments are everywhere. From your roommate refusing to do the dishes, to long strings of comments on Facebook, to the look your dog gives you when you have something she wants, arguments are an important way we interact with one another. They are as common as the air we breathe. Arguments can be found in round-table discussions; at the dinner table; in narrative writing, expository writing and descriptive writing; in speeches; in court hearings; in parliamentary debate; and so on. In fact, it could be said that life is one long argument; from the moment we are born, we are arguing with someone or something. There is no respite, so we might as well enjoy the challenge of a good argument and learn how we can benefit from it individually and collectively.

Where society and science are concerned, argumentation is not a zero-sum activity with a winner and a loser. Rather argumentation is how society grows and evolves into something better. And as I've said above, more important than devising and delivering a good argument is the ability to *hear* a well-reasoned argument. Being able to argue and to win arguments is certainly satisfying and important. And there is no question that argument is essential to establishing whether or not an idea, a course of action, a personal decision, or a government policy is good for us. But as the eighteenth- and nineteenth-century essayist and moralist Joseph Joubert once wrote in his *Pensées* (Thoughts), "The aim of argument, or of discussion, should not be victory, but progress."

Does all argumentation lead to better outcomes? Experience and history tell us that better outcomes can never be guaranteed; however, argumentation can improve the likelihood of making good decisions on the basis of what is true and real.

Why does argumentation make decisions better? Nowhere is the collaborative aspect of argumentation more evident than when we examine how human beings perceive things, and how they turn their individual perception of reality into collective knowledge. **Perception** is a primary feature of human experience; it is the *faculty of perceiving or the intuitive recognition of a truth.* The answer to the question how argumentation makes dealing with reality better may come from the universal truth that it is impossible for any one person to perceive all of reality at once.

The simple fact is that in our three-dimensional universe, our senses are limited and incapable of taking in and processing all of the available data and the perspectives on that data. We often need each other's help to grasp the complexities of reality and to sort what is true from what is false. In his examination of how humans "understand," the famous eighteenth-century philosopher, David Hume, offers some insights into the difficulty of capturing reality:

> When we look about us towards external objects, and consider the operation of causes, we are never able, in a single instance, to discover any power or necessary connexion; any quality, which binds the effect to the cause, and renders the one an infallible consequence of the other. There is required a medium, which may enable the mind to draw such an inference, if indeed it be drawn by reasoning and argument. What that medium is, I must confess, passes my comprehension; and it is incumbent on those to produce it, who assert that it really exists, and is the origin of all our conclusions concerning matter of fact. This question I propose as much for the sake of information, as with an intention of raising difficulties. I cannot find, I cannot imagine any such reasoning. But I keep my mind still open to instruction, if any one will vouchsafe to bestow it upon me.[11]

As Hume suggests, we not be able to understand fully why the universe is the way it is, but we do need to devise methods and mechanisms for dealing with reality and to open our minds to its possibilities.

The following exercise illustrates how complex an understanding of our three-dimensional reality can be and tells us how much we rely on others for our understanding of life and of reality. This is why the concept of *perspective* carries so much meaning in everyday language. **Perspective** is *the apparent relation between visible objects as to position or distance, or a point of view, or a way of regarding a matter.*

REALITY CHECK

Exercise: The Importance of Perspective to Understanding Reality

With three or more friends, colleagues, or fellow students, stand around a single object, such as a table, at various angles and distances.

Pretend you have never seen a table before, try to take it all in, and take your turn *describing precisely.*

You will quickly realize that if you look at the table from where you stand (from your "perspective") you will always lose sight of one or more aspects of the table: if you look at the table top, you will lose sight of the underside of the table, some of the edges of the table, or even one or more of the legs. If you look at the table from below you lose sight of the top. If you look at the table from one side, you may lose sight of one, two, or three sides. And looking at the surface of the table very closely may mean losing sight of the actual essence of what makes the table a table. One person might see damage to the table that may make it unsuitable for use, and so on. Personal characteristics such as colour blindness, visual impairments, and height may come into play.

Every person "experiences" the table differently. Perspective really does matter: it gives you one reality, but as a critical thinker, you also understand that others have their own reality. You need to make assumptions and feel comfortable with not "knowing" all there is to know about reality. In truth, you "know" that your understanding of the table is incomplete and can be better when others contribute their views on a matter.

As we consider the implications of the "Reality Check" exercise above and the importance of perspective to our understanding of reality, we should also consider that other people's opinions (perspectives) do matter. Seeking advice, researching, discussing, arguing, and debating are activities that increase our understanding of reality, and each one has the potential to ease the experience of navigating through life.

Not all advice is equal, however. In fact, some of the highest salaries in the world are paid to those who are considered **experts**, which literally means *a person trained by experience*, but also to those who know how to argue. Lawyers, for example, command some of the highest fees because they are skilled at argumentation. And any person wanting to be considered a professional (an expert) in this globalized economy must know how to communicate effectively and to persuade through argumentation. If we look at the most authoritative resource on occupations in Canada, the National Occupational Classification (NOC), or the Dictionary of Occupational Titles (DOT) in the United States, we find that the verbal skill required for professions such as lawyer, doctor, and business executive, who are some of the highest-paid professionals in most capitalist countries, are in the "superior" range. Once again, one is left to conclude that a person who argues well tends to live well, and that a person who argues poorly is likely to live less well.

Arguments influence decisions, public policy, and public spending. Good arguments can change and have changed the course of history. People have been known to make sacrifices willingly, even give up their lives, for causes that were well argued. Conversely, simplistic, poorly researched, and irrational arguments can have bad consequences for individuals and for society. How do we separate good arguments from bad? And are good arguments a guarantee against bad decisions? For answers to those questions, we need to look in more detail at politics and the role that argument plays in our lives, as well as the ways in which argumentation has been refined to improve the quality of our lives.

Quality of Life: Why Researching, Writing, and Debating Matter in Politics

The next time someone gives you their opinion about a politician or a political event, ask them to define *politics*. We all have opinions about politics and politicians, but you may be surprised by just how few of us can actually give a useful definition of politics. The fact that so few citizens (that is, people who have the right to vote and elect those who govern on our behalf) are unable to define politics is not only astonishing but frightening. Why, in a democracy, do our politicians and our educational system allow or even perpetuate ignorance and uncritical thinking about something so vital to our well-being? Some may argue that an uninformed and uninvolved public is much easier to manipulate. A proper definition of what we mean when we say "politics" is vital to our understanding of why research, writing, and debating matter to civilized life. For instance, the most widely used definitions of politics are based on those of the famous Canadian-born political scientist David Easton, who observed in the 1950s that societies must find a way of allocating values in order to function. Easton defined politics as *the authoritative allocation of values* for a society. Over the years political scientists have modified that definition to suit their own theoretical needs and to clarify the meaning. For instance, Easton's use of the word "values" may be a

REALITY CHECK

A Useful Definition of Politics

Defining politics is a complex business. While all the definitions below offer insight into the nature of politics, one or two of them might be more suited to your task. Which of these definitions makes most sense to you and why?

Politics is not a science. . . . Politics is the art of the possible. (Attributed to Otto von Bismarck, circa 1863.)

Politics is the activity by which the framework of human life is sustained. (Kenneth Minogue, 1995.)

Politics is the art of preventing people from taking part in affairs which properly concern them. (Paul Valéry, 1943)

Politics—a strife of interests masquerading as a contest of principles. The conduct of public affairs for private advantage. (Ambrose Bierce, 1906)[12]

little too broad or vague, and so some political scientists have added the allocation of "resources" as well as values.

For the purposes of this guide, which is to examine research, writing, and debating in politics and also its importance to our quality of life, I would like to suggest that we modify the definition even further and add a little more of description of what politics is really about. **Politics** will be defined as a *human activity for managing power and for resolving conflict over values and resources.* By **values** I mean *a belief in what is important or ethical or is a priority for a person or for society.* And by **resources** I mean *anything that can be used by society, such as money, people, property, and raw resources, to achieve an end.*

The on-going need to resolve conflict over resources and values means that societies are by their very nature *political.* And if we look at all of the passionate arguments that take place at your dinner table, in school classrooms, and in the legislatures of any functional nation-state, it is clear that they belong in one of two categories: *values* and *resources.* It also follows that the manner in which decisions are made and the consequences of those decisions for the members of that society are inextricably linked. Good arguments do matter.

As we determine which definition is best suited to understanding the value of argumentation in politics and of persuasion over coercion, let us consider what philosophers have said about the characteristics of *good politics*. For example, Lao Tzu, the fourth-century BCE Chinese philosopher, noted, "How cautious is the Sage, how sparing of his words! When his task is accomplished and affairs are prosperous, the people all say: 'We have come to be as we are, naturally and of ourselves.'"[13]

Philosophers such as Plato and Aristotle frequently commented on the nature of politics and its importance to how well society functioned. Plato believed that justice should be the prevailing social value and that competing interests could be harmonized if the society was arranged in a way that was just.[14] Aristotle, on the other hand, defined politics as "things concerning the polis" (or the political community) and thought that the human being was by nature "a political animal."[15]

In his treatise on politics, Aristotle suggested that living well in society requires an understanding of how the elements of a good life—friendship, wealth, virtue, and honour—fit together in the political community to create happiness in *the people*. When politics are not well managed, that is, not governed for the common good, *the people* suffer. Note that Aristotle did not think highly of democracy, which he said was government by the needy, and that it was a less than satisfactory arrangement. He classified political arrangements (regimes) according to whether they ruled for private interests or the common good.

Max Weber, one of the founders of the social sciences, wrote in his 1919 essay "Politics as a Vocation," that politics was the art of compromise and decision making on the basis of social benefits. He believed that politicians should embrace an ethical code that appreciates the ultimate social consequences of their actions. In other words, politicians should have a strong sense of civic responsibility.[16]

But what can politics do to achieve the greater good and make people happy? It seems that in essence good politics does two things:

1. First, it provides a way for society to *manage power* in such a way as to prevent those who wield power from abusing it.

2. And second, it helps society *manage conflict*. Conflict typically occurs over two things:

   a. claims relating to scarce *resources*; and

   b. claims about *values*.

Where does political conflict arise? According to David Easton, there are two significant types of political conflict: conflict over values (for example, disputes over social direction or ethical matters such as a woman's right to choose whether or not to remain pregnant, the right to assisted suicide, or gay rights) and conflict over resources (such as disputes over property ownership, division of assets, water rights, and taxation).[17]

Why is persuasion better than authority and coercion? As was pointed out above, persuasion allows us to act in an atmosphere of security and allows the members of the community to use collaboration rather than coercion to achieve the common good. In a political system where coercion is used to achieve social ends, much of society's energy and resources is diverted to threatening or to carrying out a threat. And the external threat must be ever-present for the general population to be motivated to act or behave in the way approved by the state. On the other hand, great things can be accomplished when the impetus to act a certain way comes from within each individual. Canada's extraordinary effort in both world wars is a good example of what a society can accomplish when the citizens are motivated from within.

In a political system where persuasion is used to achieve social ends, the energy is expended instead at arriving at the best possible solution with the greatest amount of collaboration between the citizens and the state. To learn more about the process of persuasion in civilized society, we should look at how research, writing, and debating are used in the act of persuasion.

Argumentation and the Phases of Researching, Writing, and Debating

What an actual argument looks like in abstract terms, is conveyed in Figure I.1. Every argument makes a claim that must be supported effectively by **evidence**.

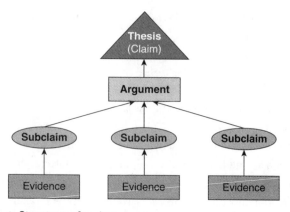

Figure I.1 ⊚ Structure of an Argument

Argumentation in the hard sciences and the social sciences, including political science, has evolved to the point where a standard approach can be used. And the research and writing process is a cycle that can be repeated over and over. As Figure I.2 suggests, preparing an argument, writing an essay, or presenting research in political science and other scientific endeavours typically follows a common set of steps or stages, also known as a process, with a specific methodology for achieving clarity of meaning and maintaining the quality of the collected data.

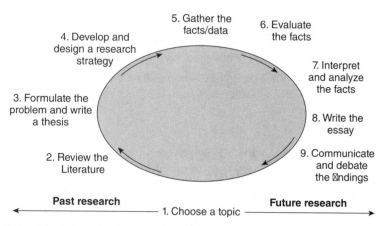

Figure I.2 ⊚ Steps for Researching, Writing, and Debating in the Social Sciences

These steps can save time and effort, but more importantly, the process helps to ensure that the arguments are well-founded and supported with factual evidence, that the arguments are delivered in a format that is comprehensible to other people, and finally, that the arguments can be used to advance human knowledge and civilization.

The following is a summary of these steps:

1. Choose a general topic in your field of study.
2. Conduct preliminary research by reviewing the literature.
3. Ask questions, formulate the problem, and write a thesis (a pro or con statement that makes a *claim*). (This is a good time to use the Seneca Libraries worksheet posted at www.oupcanada.com/Menard).
4. Design your research to explore the problem.
5. Gather the facts (evidence or data), and make sure you keep track of all of your sources.
6. Assess and evaluate the collected facts and analyze the facts: i.e., explain the evidence or data, and make connections between the research and your thesis.
7. Interpret data and define the topic.
8. Write the essay.
9. Publish, present, or debate your findings.

Each step is discussed in greater detail in the chapters that follow. Part I addresses the research process, its scientific aspects, the strategies to follow, and pitfalls to avoid. Part II discusses the nature of the essay, the writing process, and the best ways of structuring an argument. And finally, Part III explores the art and science of debating.

Conclusion

If we accept that **politics** is *a human activity for the management of power and conflict*, and that the activity of politics has the potential for making citizens happier and life more civilized, then surely a skill that helps manage conflict and power in a civilized way should be encouraged in our society and our educational system. In fact, rational argumentation is a skill that should be prized in the public's consciousness along with other human skills such as making fire, growing food, and healing the sick.

After reading this introduction, the reader should have an appreciation of how important argumentation is to our security and our quality of life, and should realize that not all arguments are bad for us. In fact, societies can control conflict and power for the common good and allow argumentation to take place in structured and peaceful ways that allow for the energy of conflicts to be harnessed constructively. This guide to research, writing, and debating will continue to examine the nature of argumentation and show ways in which argumentation can be used to maintain civilized life.

Review Exercises

1. In a liberal democracy, which institutions are essential to the protection of the right to argue peacefully? Explain how these institutions and rights work and why they matter.
2. Go to freedomhouse.org and compare the level of freedom in liberal democracies in the Americas, which have an average freedom score of 71 per cent, with the countries of Eurasia, which have an average score of 0 per cent. How much of this score is related to the protection or the suppression of institutions that allow free speech and argumentation?
3. How many arguments have you had this week? What was the nature of those arguments (abusive or civil)? Were they arguments about resources or values?

PART I

Researching

1 The Importance of Research in Political Argument

There is not a discovery in science, however revolutionary, however sparkling with insight that does not arise out of what went before. "If I have seen further than other men," said Isaac Newton, "it is because I have stood on the shoulders of giants."

—Isaac Asimov, *Adding a Dimension*

The saying "Garbage in, garbage out" is commonly used in reference to the quality of a product or service. It means that when you use inferior materials in the creation of any product or service, be they cooked dishes, or home renovations, or inadequate medications in a course of medical treatment, the end result is also likely to be inferior. The same may be said of political arguments, essays, or debates, where much depends on the quality of the materials used in their creation. How one approaches, structures, and conducts the examination of what is "garbage" and what is not is likely to affect the quality of the argument. The process by which we familiarize ourselves with the subject matter and separate what is useful from what is not, is called research. This chapter offers a "how-to" approach to designing and conducting research, which is based on the underlying principles of political science. And perhaps as importantly, it explains why these research techniques matter to the quality of the argument.

A successful argument in poltics and political science, oral or written communication contains the right balance of style and of substance.

And so, political writing and debating requires the skills of **rhetoric**, which is *the art of effective or persuasive speaking or writing*, as well as research skills. And the research we conduct must be done in accordance with certain scientific methods and principles such as those found in political science. This chapter is devoted to the research aspect of debating and writing in politics and political science.

What Is Research?

Nothing about **research** is dreamy or exciting, and that includes the definition: *the systematic investigation into and study of materials, sources, etc. in order to establish facts and reach new conclusion.* The words "fun" and "research" are seldom seen in the same sentence. In fact, the very mention of the word usually elicits glassy stares, yawns, and a surge of bodies heading towards the exits. Many students are surprised to hear me refer to research as a "creative process," and even more surprised to hear that research is at the very heart of the creative process. Those who take research seriously stand a better chance of achieving success than those who do not. That applies to school, to business, and to society at large.

It may come as a shock to many, but creation is not happenstance. One of the myths about great art is that it just happens, and that great artists, be they writers, painters, or musicians, are born with an ability to produce great works, an ability that the rest of us aren't born with. As an experienced teacher, I have to say that this . . . is utter nonsense. Even those who have talent must train and work to become proficient. Ask any successful visual artist, for example, and they will tell you that research and hard work are the key to making a successful piece of art or putting together a successful exhibition.

Research does many things:

⊙   solves problems
⊙   confirms, reconfirms, or disconfirms facts
⊙   determines the validity of a theory or a test
⊙   discovers new fields of research

- ⊚ expands the field of knowledge
- ⊚ documents a process
- ⊚ helps us interpret what we perceive

However, the most important thing that research gives us is **knowledge**, i.e., *a theoretical and practical understanding of a subject.* Note that the kind of understanding referred to here is the "theoretical and practical" kind and not the kind that comes from intuition.

The Enlightenment philosopher and scientist Sir Francis Bacon is credited with the famous phrase "Knowledge is power." Knowledge makes us powerful because it not only helps us describe what is being observed or experienced but also increases our awareness of and familiarity (our understanding) with the subject matter; in turn, mastery of the subject matter can give us **implicit knowledge**, that is, *practical skills*, or **explicit knowledge**, that is, *theoretical understanding*. Knowledge can help us distinguish what is factual from what is not, and thus give us what we need to make the best decisions possible—decisions that are most likely to be correct. Finally, for the purposes of this book, knowledge can help us develop rational, sound, and persuasive arguments.

Knowledge, or what Plato called "justified true belief," is a complex process involving the human faculties of perception, reasoning, and communication. This is belief that goes beyond what our intuition and our emotions tell us about reality. In fact, there is an entire field of philosophical study called epistemology, which is dedicated entirely to "how we know things." **Epistemology** has a number of definitions, including *the study of knowledge, the theory of knowledge* and also as *the science of science.* Much of what is written here about research in political science is directly related to epistemology and what it can tell us about the treatment of political science as a science and about the benefits and the pitfalls of scientific research, particularly in the social sciences.

Depending on one's field of study, research can take many forms. And as we will see below in the discussion of the science in political science and the differences between the so-called hard sciences and the soft sciences, the research methods may vary significantly from one field of study to another. Nevertheless, for proper research to take place, some basic principles must be followed.

Valuing the "Science" in Political Science

That the study of politics should be considered a science is not without its detractors. Many famous people have referred to politics as an art. One of them was French essayist, poet, and philosopher Paul Valéry, who wrote in 1943, "*Politics is the art of preventing people from taking part in affairs which properly concern them.*" To some, like Valéry, even if you collected all the facts about a subject, you might never understand the art of it. Political science is often referred to as a "liberal arts" discipline, which suggests that its study leads to a broad, general knowledge, but not the kind of education that would give a person applied or how-to knowledge or a trade. Indeed, politics is not plumbing. Over the years many academics have remarked that political science relies far too much on **generalizations** (*a proposition or general notion that is based on limited or inadequate cases*) to be properly considered a science. And after all, how can a man-made invention, with no "right" or "wrong" answers, be properly called a science? And what is meant by the term "science"?

What I have always appreciated about political science courses is that they helps your knowledge as a citizen in three ways. First, political science is an amalgamation of many different disciplines, including psychology, economics, culture, geography, history, law, games theory, and science; therefore its study, like that of other liberal arts courses, will give you breadth of knowledge about society and your place in it. Second, political science empowers you as a citizen by showing you how society functions and how you can effect change at all levels. This includes influencing outcomes through persuasive argument. And finally, you learn about political science as a discipline, which includes the principles of critical thinking, the conventions of oral and written communication, the scientific and ethical principles behind the research, and the skills needed to present and publish these findings.

Again, there are many definitions and complexities associated with science; some definitions would exclude political science; others would include it. For example, the *Oxford Canadian Dictionary*'s first definition of **science**, if strictly applied, might exclude political science: *a branch of knowledge conducted on objective principles involving the systematized observation of and experiments with phenomena, [especially] concerned* *with the material and functions of the physical universe.* This last part can present a special kind of problem for political scientists who study, for example, voter behaviour. A more inclusive definition for political scientists might be Oxford's second definition: *systematic and formulated knowledge*; and third definition: *an organized body of knowledge on a subject.* Any one of those definitions will suit our purpose.

One could say that treating politics as something that could be studied as a science probably started some 2,500 years ago with Greek philosophers such as Plato and Aristotle, whose preoccupation with creating or identifying the characteristics of the ideal society formed the basis of their study. Plato and Aristotle developed concepts and methods for studying politics that are still in use today. For example, Aristotle's *taxonomy* of states and constitutions is discussed in Chapter 4; taxonomies are a most useful scientific device for comparing the qualities and characteristics of a specific class of items, in this case states and constitutions.

Similarly, the eighteenth-century Scottish philosopher David Hume argued that the study of politics should be considered a science so that those who govern would know which forms of government are best. In his essay "That Politics May be Reduced to a Science," Hume writes

It is a question with several, whether there be any essential difference between one form of government and another? and, whether every form may not become good or bad, according as it is well or ill administered? Were it once admitted, that all governments are alike, and that the only difference consists in the character and conduct of the governors, most political disputes would be at an end, and all *Zeal* for one constitution above another, must be esteemed mere bigotry and folly. But, though a friend to moderation, I cannot forbear condemning this sentiment, and should be sorry to think, that human affairs admit of no greater stability, than what they receive from the casual humours and characters of particular men.

And also,

It may therefore be pronounced as an universal axiom in politics, That an hereditary prince, a nobility without vassals, and a

people voting by their representatives, form the best MONAR-
CHY, ARISTOCRACY, and DEMOCRACY. But in order to prove
more fully, that politics admit of general truths, which are in-
variable by the humour or education either of subject or sovereign, it may not be amiss to observe some other principles of
this science, which may seem to deserve that character.[1]

To Hume, good government was not a simple matter of personalities or
of humour—the moods, temperaments, or education of those in government and of those being governed—but a matter of scientific study with
specific principles to apply and methods to follow.

In 1895, the French sociologist and philosopher Émile Durkheim
pioneered the field of the social sciences with his *Rules of Methodolog-
ical Research*. Durkheim made an important and lasting connection
between knowledge in the natural sciences and knowledge of what happens in society.

Durkheim ... conceived of a domain of the social, distinct from
other orders of reality, but no less a reality in its own right. . . .
[He] advocated the foundation of a scientific knowledge of
this domain which would resemble the natural sciences in its
approach and forms of explanation. The new science, in theo-
rising the conditions of social order, had a necessary political
role in preventing anarchy and social disintegration.[2]

And, as in all sciences, in order to prevent scientific knowledge from
becoming **dogma**, that is, *a belief or set of beliefs held by an authority
or group, which others are expected to accept without argument* (i.e., an
arrogant declaration of opinion), scientists and citizens need to understand that the quest for knowledge can never stop; all perspectives
and approaches must be considered. Feminist scholars of the twenti-
eth century, for instance, made it possible for political scientists to see
how male-centric dogma or epistemologies could be used to rationalize
prejudice and discrimination at home, in the workplace, and in politics.
The feminist slogan of the 1960s "the political is personal" says that our
political relations and institutions could contain the seeds of bias and
discrimination and result in harmful social inequalities.

Again, the purpose of following scientific methods and principles is be to improve our understanding and to arrive at the best solutions and best forms of governance for the common good. This invites the question: can science be used to improve the quality of argumentation in the quest for better governance? And what makes one argument better than another? To answer those questions, we need to explore another area of human knowledge: rhetoric.

Rhetoric and Science

As mentioned above, *rhetoric is the art of effective or persuasive speaking or writing*, and it is rhetoric that makes public speaking and debating an art form and thus an instrument of political change. Those who are skilled at rhetoric, as we will see in Chapter 5, are able to harness the power of language and, therefore, have the use of a powerful tool for changing people's behaviour and of moving people to acts of greatness but also to acts of inhumanity and barbarity. Without a good grounding in rhetoric, ethics, and the principles of science on the part of both the rhetorician and the audience, a sense of what is meant by "true justified belief," the audience may be prone to believe anything a good public speaker says, and consequently rhetoric can easily fall into the dark side of argumentation and persuasion. The result is then **sophistry**, which is *the use of intentionally deceptive or specious arguments or reasoning*. Rhetoric seeks to teach students how to balance emotional appeal with critical reasoning. It seems logical and socially desirable, therefore, for any twenty-first-century education to include some training on the difference between a rational argument and sophistry.

Some early Greek philosophers and teachers, called Sophists, saw rhetoric as having a great potential for social good, and the teaching of oration and of rhetorical skills became very popular around 450 BCE. But the term "Sophist" eventually developed a negative connotation because of the capacity of rhetoric to be used for evil as well as for good. The Sophists soon became the subject of a parody by the Greek playwright, Aristophanes, who thought Sophists had the ability to use language to deceive and to manipulate. Over the centuries, many writers and philosophers have commented on rhetoric's darker side. For instance,

Richard Whately, a nineteenth-century Anglican archbishop of Dublin, educator, logician, and social reformer, wrote, "Sophistry is like a window curtain—it pleases as an ornament, but its true use is to keep out the light." And the nineteenth-century poet Samuel Taylor Coleridge wrote, "The juggle of sophistry consists, for the most part, in using a word in one sense in the premises, and in another sense in the conclusion." Indeed, without the proper application of scientific methods and critical reasoning as well as ethics, there is danger of rhetoric's becoming sophistry and illusion. Therefore, rhetoric needs to be tempered with reason, science, and ethics in order for it to serve the greater good. But it is equally important that both the listener and the deliverer of the message have a certain amount of education in rhetoric and in critical thinking or science in order to appreciate and be persuaded by a good argument.

Exactly what the rhetorical skills are and how to apply them will be the subject of the final chapter of this guide. But first we will look at the scientific principles of research in fields like political science.

Research and Turning "Barroom Guesses" into "Educated Guesses"

Did you ever wonder what the difference is between a "barroom guess" and an "educated guess"? Probably not, but everyone has made their share of barroom guesses, as well as educated guesses. In fact, if you listen carefully to the social interactions that people have with family, friends, colleagues, and strangers, you will notice that barroom guesses and educated guesses are part of everyday conversation.

Barroom guesses are *groundless opinions and predictions that are not based on fact.* For example, predicting that your favourite team will win a sports championship is often a barroom guess, especially if you haven't done your research. Why does that matter? It matters because doing research and analysis considerably improves the reliability of our guesses and the chances of predicting outcomes correctly. A scientist's job is to use the scientific method (that is, research that includes systematic investigation and experimentation) to understand how things work so as to predict outcomes. Science can never be 100 per cent accurate in predicting outcomes, but, if used correctly, science can enable us to make *educated guesses* so as to anticipate problems, improve outcomes, reduce risks, and improve the quality of our decisions. **Educated guesses** are *opinions and predictions based on factual evidence.*

Properly conducted research—research that is conducted ethically and according to scientific methods and principles—improves the quality of our knowledge in two ways: by making the data (1) more **reliable**, that is, *dependable, and of sound and consistent character and quality*; and (2) valid, that is, *sound, well-founded, and defensible.* These are two concepts important to scientific research and methods, as well as to rhetoric and argumentation, that will be discussed in more detail in Chapter 2.

Nevertheless, even with research, a prediction can never be more than an educated guess. Why is that? It is because of the application of a basic principle of scientific knowledge called *induction.*

Induction is *the inference of a particular law from particular instances.* In other words, if we observe a particular event often enough under the same set of conditions, we can infer the presence of a general law, which may allow us to predict certain outcomes. We can and do call this "knowledge"; however, this knowledge is never more than a probable estimate or an approximation of what is happening or what could happen. Bertrand Russell, a well-regarded twentieth-century philosopher who explored, among other things, the sciences and how we "know" things, wrote:

> Although this may seem a paradox, all exact science is dominated by the idea of approximation. When a man tells you that he knows the exact truth about anything, you are safe in inferring that he is an inexact man. Every careful measurement in science is always given with the probable error . . . every observer admits that he is likely wrong, and knows about how much wrong he is likely to be.[3]

Therefore, the purpose of a social science, such as political science, is to make the best, most realistic approximations about society. And the job of the political scientist is to explain what has happened and what is happening and to predict what could happen. For example, a political scientist who studies international relations might explain the root causes of the phenomenon we call "globalization," explain what global-ization looks like today, and also try to predict what globalization might look like in the future.

Of course, educated guesses tend to be made less frequently than barroom guesses because there is work involved in making sure that the explanation of events and any relevant predictions are as accurate as possible. Educated guesses take patience, time, and resources. As pointed out above, if political scientists can only make *educated guesses*, then they should never claim to know anything with absolute certain-ty. Caution, discipline, and humility are qualities that any scientist, but especially political scientists, must cultivate. As Eoin Colfer remarked in *Artemis Fowl*, "Confidence is ignorance. If you're feeling cocky, it's be-cause there's something you don't know." In his *Problems of Philosophy* (1912), Bertrand Russell examines this particular problem of induction in science and knowledge:

> The belief that the sun will rise tomorrow might be falsified if the earth came suddenly into contact with a large body which destroyed its rotation; but the laws of motion and the law of gravitation would not be infringed by such an event. The business of science is to find uniformities, such as the laws of motion and the law of gravitation, to which, so far as our expe-rience extends, there are no exceptions. In this search science has been remarkably successful, and it may be conceded that such uniformities have held hitherto. This brings us back to the question: Have we any reason, assuming that they have always held in the past, to suppose that they will hold in the future?[4]

So, if absolute certainty is not possible, then what is possible? Stu-dents of political science eventually learn that research not only deep-ens their understanding of a subject matter but also improves their chances of understanding society and, to a limited extent, of predicting outcomes. The great irony here is that a political scientist must become comfortable with the feeling of insecurity that comes from not knowing everything for certain. It is the acceptance of insecurity as a natural fact that makes political scientists humble, flexible, and open to new ideas.

REALITY CHECK

In case of smugness, read the following:

"The greatest enemy of knowledge is not ignorance, it is the illusion of knowledge."—Daniel J. Boorstin

"Without education, we are in a horrible and deadly danger of taking educated people seriously."—G.K. Chesterton

"It's an universal law—intolerance is the first sign of an inadequate education. An ill-educated person behaves with arrogant impatience, whereas truly profound education breeds humility."—Aleksandr Solzhenitsyn

"You are not entitled to your opinion. You are entitled to your *informed* opinion. No one is entitled to be ignorant."—Harlan Ellison[5]

Natural (Hard) Sciences versus Social (Soft) Sciences

What are the differences between the natural sciences and the social sciences? Why do these differences matter?

The natural sciences (the hard sciences) and the social sciences (also known as the "soft" sciences) have many similarities. For one thing, they believe in the importance of factual evidence. All sciences have at their core the belief that by using certain techniques, one can explain what has happened in the past and, with that knowledge, predict what can reasonably be expected in the future. Observation and the gathering of **empirical data** (i.e., *information collected through the senses*) are at the very heart of all scientific activities. Consequently, both the natural and the social sciences use similar principles and practices in the study of nature and the universe.

Another way of saying this is that scientists gather factual evidence, through empirical observation, in order to prove or disprove a thesis. Natural sciences research methods include observation and experimentation, which are also used in the social sciences. However, the natural sciences are believed to be more objective than social sciences because there is less change and fewer exceptions to the rule. For example, if we look at some of the great modern structures such as New York's Empire State Building, or Toronto's Bloor Viaduct, we note that these achievements were possible because engineers used scientific knowledge developed over hundreds of years and applied this knowledge with close to absolute certainty. In the social sciences, however, such certainty is far less likely—some might say virtually impossible. Why must the political scientist be comfortable with a significant but reasonable amount of uncertainty? The main reason is that the social sciences study human beings. Unlike inanimate and many other animate objects, humans are said to be sentient beings and are able to think and able to communicate. Humans are not static or inanimate: they are mobile and they are changeable. Compare that to a rock, which, as far as we know, does not feel, think, or communicate. Or again, think of a virus or lichen, which are life forms which use problem-solving techniques that do not require either a brain or communication techniques.

Perhaps another distinguishing characteristic of the social sciences is that their methods include significant *qualitative* rather than a *quantitative* elements. (See Table 1.1.) Something is considered **qualitative** when it is about *anything that is not quantitative, verifiable, or subject to measurement.* On the other hand, a discipline is considered **quantitative** when it *studies an aspect of reality as something that can be measured and verified.* For example, political scientists often look at numbers and the measurable, and the science of collecting and analyzing numerical data is called *statistics.* Statistics focuses mainly on what can be measured and extrapolated from those measurements; in political science we use them to measure and understand social change.

The qualitative aspect of the social sciences often leads political scientists to express *opinions* on the significance or importance of a social phenomenon without their opinions being based on something that can be measured. Here, we must distinguish between opinion and informed opinion. An **opinion** *is a belief or assessment based on grounds short of proof, or a view held as probable.* **Informed opinion**, on the other hand, *is a belief*

Table 1.1 ⊚ Differences between Qualitative and Quantitative Research

	Research Methodology	
	Qualitative	Quantitative
Purpose *Why are we doing the research and the analysis?*	To discover one or more ideas or concepts.	To test a hypothesis or answer specific questions.
Approach *What is the methodology?*	Methods yield data that are personal and subjective, but that provide an opportunity to explore meaning, depth, and nuance.	Methods yield data that are based on objective observation.
Data Collection Techniques and Interpretation	Subjective data is obtained by seeking, observing, and interpreting subjective experience.	Objective data is obtained by testing, measurement, and experimentation.
How is data being collected and interpreted?	Subjective data is explained as it relates to the individual or to the collective.	For the data to be useful, it must be *reliable* and *valid*. The researcher must be able to explain how the data was arrived at and show that the methods were reliable and valid.
Independence *What is the writer's or researcher's level of involvement?*	The observer is not necessarily detached from the information-collecting process; therefore, the results are more personal and subjective.	The observer is detached so that the results are objective.
Sampling	Sample size is less relevant to the outcome or may not be relevant at all.	Reasonable-sized sample is necessary to allow the researcher to make generalizations, inferences, and predictions.

formed on the basis of fact. For example, a political scientist might examine the qualities and characteristics of ideologies such as liberalism, conservatism, or socialism, and speculate (offer an opinion) on their importance in an upcoming election. Or he or she might examine how political institutions such as the Canadian Parliament, the bureaucracy, or the Supreme Court might be looked at with respect to their effects on Canadian society. As much as possible, a social scientist must try to explain the social reality by looking at the **facts**—*something that can be measured or verified*—rather than the subjective opinions and values of those being studied—For our purposes, a value is *a belief in what is important or ethical.*

Although the qualitative approach gives the writer the opportunity to explain why things matter from a personal or a social standpoint, a political scientist who is too qualitative in his or her analysis and strays too far from what is "measurable" might be accused of not being factual and labelled "unscientific." A political scientist might be considered unscientific if, for example, he or she made a generalization like this one: "Canadians believe that we should have a democratically elected Senate in Ottawa. Therefore, the Prime Minister should appoint only democratically elected Senators." Without the research to prove the claim of what Canadians believe about the Senate and more research and analysis into the viable or desirable options with respect to the Canadian Senate, this claim is unscientific. In short, political scientists should strive to establish clearly what *is* before offering solutions to socio-political problems or expressing opinions on what *ought* to happen. Again, the first and most important step in the process is to describe and explain the reality by looking at the facts. This is why looking for factual evidence through surveys, experimental research, or a thorough review of the literature on a given subject is so important to our arguments.

The Phases of Research

Hopefully, the discussion above has put us in the proper frame of mind for discussing the phases of research in the social sciences, including political science.

Selecting a Topic and Preliminary Research

The first step in the process of research, writing, and debating is to choose a topic and write the thesis. In fact, that may be the most important task. Why is that?

Not only is the thesis the starting point but it also defines the direction, scope, and strategies and methodologies to be used in collecting the data needed to write the essay. At the master's and doctorate levels, a great deal of time and energy is spent at the beginning in writing the thesis to avoid wasting time and energy in the actual research phase.

At the undergraduate or college level, students are often given a general topic or a list of topics to choose from. If you have the opportunity to choose your own topic or are given a list of topics to choose from, you should keep the following in mind:

1. Read the course outline and the course learning outcomes so that the topic you choose is relevant.
2. The length of the essay is an important indicator of what is manageable in terms of research and of writing. You don't want to bite off more than you can chew.
3. Check with the professor, the library, and the Internet for available resources.
4. Determine the type of research that will be required. As a first step, use the resources and tools made available through the local library. An example of one of the worksheets can be seen in Appendix I, available at www.oupcanada.com/Menard.

Here are more guidelines and ideas for selecting an essay topic:

1. Choose something you are interested in. People tend to do better at tasks they are interested in.
2. Brainstorm with fellow students.
3. Draw a **mind map**. (A mind map is a drawing or diagram to represent and organize the ideas, images, and words connected to a single concept.)
4. Ask a librarian.
5. Consult your professor.
6. Do preliminary research.

Once you have selected your topic and done some preliminary research, write a draft thesis statement. At the master's or doctorate level, a thesis may include:

⊚   A brief introduction that presents the general question you want to ask and answer.

⊚   A brief explanation of the relevance of your proposed research to the body of knowledge in your subject area.

⊚   A summary of some of the past research and writings with some explanation of how your research will differ.

⊚   A brief description of the research methods and the scope or boundaries of your study.

⊚   A conclusion that highlights the importance of the research to the field of study and how your research might lead others to continue.

⊚   A summary of the references used in the development of your thesis.

In short, to avoid wasting time, energy, or even physical or financial resources, you must do research about doing your research. Certain activities, such as following the steps above and making mind maps of the concepts contained in the project itself and the research that needs to be conducted, might open your mind to possibilities that you had not considered. These activities may even prevent gaps from developing in the research and writing.

(N.B. It is wise at this stage of the process to lay out a plan and timetable for conducting the research and writing the essay. This will be discussed in more detail in the chapter on writing the essay.)

Writing the Thesis

What is a thesis and what is it good for? The word "thesis" comes from the Greek word *thésis*, which means placing or setting. In modern English, **thesis** means *a proposition (a claim) to be maintained or proved.*

For example, a researcher may want to argue in an essay that turning over public health care to the private sector would have dire consequences for Canadian society. Some political science writers might argue that a thesis is a statement, a simple affirmation of what you plan to write or argue, for example, "Canada should not privatize the health care system." Some debating societies call this an **affirmative**, that is, *an assertion that a thing is so.* Others may argue that the thesis should contain an affirmation as well as some explanation of why you believe the thesis to be correct, for example, "Canada should not privatize health care because to do so would compromise the social safety net." And in some cases, as in academic studies, a thesis proposal may be required;

that is a short essay for a master's or doctoral thesis that outlines in greater detail what the writer plans to write about, the research methodology, and why the thesis topic matters. A master's or doctoral thesis in this case is also known as a dissertation. For our purposes here, a thesis is a *signal that tells the reader what your intention is.*

The first step is to write a draft, or a working thesis. There is no reason the thesis statement cannot be changed after the essay has been written. In fact, writers often change their thesis and rewrite their introduction after completing their research because new evidence has changed their mind. Nevertheless, in order to ensure that the thesis is suitable for your purposes, check the thesis against the following:

⊚ The thesis must have substance or meaning for you and for your readers or listeners.
⊚ The thesis should be contestable, that is, open to discussion, and not just a statement of fact.
⊚ The thesis must be precise about a particular circumstance or issue.
⊚ The thesis must be clear; that is, the reader should be able to tell (from your introduction or your thesis proposal) exactly what you plan to argue.
⊚ The thesis makes an assertion that needs to be discussed and supported with evidence.

Thus, the essay is merely a writer's attempt at proving the thesis and, as such, most of an essay is one person's proof that his or her thesis is correct.

Research and Establishing Facts

As shown in Table 1.1, facts are the essential building blocks of any argument or essay, and the task of researching is the gathering and establishing of *facts*. A **fact** is *a thing that is known to have occurred and that exists, and that can be verified.*

Research is the foundation of any argument, and most of us have an innate sense when we are not well-prepared for an argument because we haven't done enough research. And your opponents and those in the audience (or your readers) who have some knowledge of the subject can usually tell when someone is not prepared. In many cases, even persons who have no knowledge of a topic but know how to argue can tell when an argument is poorly constructed and not based on factual evidence; they may also notice the fear that comes from feeling insecure about the topic.

After selecting a topic and writing a thesis (preliminary or otherwise), the political science writer must decide what methods to use in conducting the research. The social sciences depend on a number of methods that are similar to those of the hard sciences; they include the following:

> **Observation**: experimentation, interviews, surveys, comparative studies, and case studies.
>
> **Reading documents** such as books, articles, diaries, historical texts, biographies
>
> **Participation** in people's lives and studying them first hand. For example, anthropologists and sociologists may actually live in a particular community before writing about its language, society, or culture.

Moreover, and as will be discussed in Chapter 2, scientific research methodology implies the judicious application of ethical principles, in particular adherence to the truth and the factual reporting of what we have observed.

Primary and Secondary Sources

When a person says they are going to use "primary" sources, it often suggests direct involvement in obtaining and gathering the data or using information obtained from census data or from diaries, memoirs, books, and articles written by a person who was "living or living with the topic." In other words, the primary source was written by a person who lived through a particular event or who, like an anthropologist or sociologist, actually lived with the people he or she was studying.

Primary sources are *documents or data that have not been critically or analytically distilled or filtered in any way.* They are the original observations, artifacts, research findings, or documents that have not been digested, summarized, classified, compared, or analyzed. Examples might include artifacts in an archaeological dig, the original answers from a survey, daily weather observations, or a diary.

Secondary sources are *the product of writers, journalists, and scientists, who have used primary sources to comment on a phenomenon or trend or event.* Some secondary sources can also be used as primary sources. For example, if I want to study how historical interpretation of history changes with each generation, I would want to read historians' writings (secondary sources) on a specific topic and use them as my primary sources.

Although some college and undergraduate university students might do primary research, such as conducting a survey for market research purposes, most will use secondary sources. Secondary sources have taken primary source information and manipulated or interpreted it in some way. Secondary sources are not "new" (in the sense of being written as the events being written about were occurring), and they already contain some analysis, which should be helpful to students who are not familiar with the topic. Secondary sources can be easily obtained from a bookstore, library, or the Internet. Examples of secondary sources include:

⊚   encyclopedias
⊚   popular sources such as magazines and newspaper articles
⊚   blogs
⊚   summaries or abstracts of articles, reports, or other written works
⊚   scholarly journals
⊚   audio or video documentaries
⊚   peer-reviewed publications

Please note that some professors may not let their students use blogs or certain online encyclopedias for academic papers because the publications may not be factual and may lack academic rigour.

Conclusion

No one should underestimate the value of research in the development of persuasive arguments in essays and debates. Indeed, research is the foundation of knowledge, and it is difficult to conceive of a justified true belief without research. As suggested in the opening quotations from Isaac Asimov and Sir Isaac Newton, when we do research, it is all right to rely on what has happened before and on the expertise of others in the advancement of knowledge. Our expertise on any topic grows from learning what experts have learned before us.

This preliminary discussion about research has described the specific phases of research, along with the selection of a topic and the application of certain scientific methods and principles than enhance the reliability of the evidence and the validity of our arguments. Also explored were the differences between quantitative and qualitative knowledge. The next chapter goes into greater detail about the principles and the limits of research and about how to avoid some of the pitfalls that can weaken the quality of our evidence.

Review Exercises

1. In a group or alone, list all of the guesses you've made today. Now, divide them into two categories: barroom guesses (opinion) and educated guesses (informed opinion). What standards did you use in differentiating one from the other?

2. Find a 1,500-word news story on politics in a reputable newspaper and separate what is quantitative from what is qualitative.

3. Individually or in a group, use a large blank piece of paper, a whiteboard, or a chalkboard to create a mind map of a topic you are exploring or writing about. If you've never made a mind map, start off with a concept that is rich in meaning, for example, the concept of government or citizenship or human rights, and see where that takes you. This type of activity unleashes the creative juices, and you might be surprised at the complexity and richness of ideas that come from such an exercise. It may also guide you in your research.

4. Use a two-column chart to compare the central features of democracy and despotism. Then describe their nature in paragraph for each.

2 Research Pitfalls and How to Avoid Them

Research is formalized curiosity. It is poking and prying with a purpose.

—Zora Neale Hurston

Once we have a clear idea of the topic we want to write about, and a set of questions we want answers to, the matter of gathering and processing information arises. This is arguably the most important phase of the writing process, with many pitfalls that lead to a number of offences that political scientists and political writers could be accused of, such as these:

- lack of focus (both in the research and in the writing)
- lack of analysis or superficial analysis (not enough connections between the data and the findings and a lack of detailed explanations)
- excessive use of jargon (terms improperly defined or explained)
- sample too small for the generalizations or predictions
- weak data because of faulty methods
- improper application of theory and so on.[1]

Those offences may be avoided with a generous application of scientific methodology and critical reasoning in the research. And while it might be argued that the risk of harming persons or groups in society from falling into these pitfalls is much lower in the social sciences that in engineering or medical science, there is nonetheless a risk that shoddy or faulty social science research could lead to improper decisions by voters, politicians, policy-makers, and civil servants and thus affect society adversely.

As was explained in Chapter 1, we arrive at reasonable belief through research: research improves the probability that the evidence in support of our arguments and decisions is as accurate and reliable as possible and can be used with *confidence*. How, then, do we improve the likelihood that our research is of the highest possible quality? Which sources do we use? Where do we find these sources? Will there be enough information on the topic? How do we differentiate good-quality from poor-quality information, as well as *fact* from *opinion*? And how do we make sense of the data once we have it? These last two questions are especially important. If, indeed, humans cannot know or predict anything with 100 per cent accuracy or certainty, and all we can hope for are theories and arguments based on "reasonable belief," how can we be confident that this knowledge is accurate, reliable, or useful? What follows is a discussion of the method (the principles and the techniques) that we can follow to help ensure that the evidence we use in our essays and debates is reliable and valid.

Research methodology, which is a systematic and defined set of procedures and methods used in conducting research and which is common to all the sciences, helps ensure that the factual evidence that forms the basis of our argument is **reliable** (dependable and consistent in character and in quality) and that the methods we have used to collect that evidence are **valid** (sound, well-founded, and defensible). The concepts of reliability and validity are integral to each other. But before we examine how these scientific concepts are connected, we need to examine these research concepts separately.

Reliability

In the engineering sciences, reliability is about the life cycle of a product and its dependability. For instance, when engineers test a product, such as a car, a fridge, or a blender, they will try to determine the *probability* that the product will continue to do what it is supposed to do under a specific set of conditions. They will measure the *limits of performance* for that product to arrive at a reasonable belief about the product's performance. One could say that the engineers are trying to achieve a certain *confidence* about the product's capacity to work under normal conditions and, therefore, to draw conclusions about the product's reliability. The greater the probability that the product will perform as promised, the greater the confidence we can have in its reliability.

Similarly in the social sciences, the concept of reliability is about the *confidence* we can have that our research (or whatever experiment or survey we are conducting) will yield the same result time and again. Social scientists need to be able to test the factual evidence against reality to determine whether the facts are reliable. Social scientists regularly ask questions that relate to reasonable belief in the evidence: Can the facts be verified? Will the facts stand up to scrutiny? Can we repeat the research or experiment and achieve the same set of facts or similar results?

One of the most important reasons for documenting sources and research methodology in political science essays is to determine whether the data or factual evidence can be relied upon and whether there is any bias in the research methods that could lead to faulty conclusions. One way of determining whether the data is reliable is to repeat the research that produced the data in the first place: the more often we see a political phenomenon, the better able we are to make general predictions about possible outcomes. And so, the more societies a particular phenomenon is observed in, the more reliable the observation can be considered. In comparative politics, for example, we may compare the interaction of the judiciary with the other branches of government in different political systems. If we see similarities in that interaction in three or four political systems, this data may make it possible for us to make generalizations and reliable predictions that apply to other political systems.

Reliability is also important to statistics and to surveys. For example, the reliability of a voter survey could be tested by comparing survey results with past surveys or with surveys by other pollsters. Or we could determine the reliability of the survey by randomly polling voters in the street to see if these random responses are indeed similar to the survey's predicted outcomes. If they are not, then the survey may not reliable.

These examples show what we look for in terms of reliability; however, as we will discuss in the next section, *reliability alone does not make something valid nor is something that is valid necessarily reliable.*

Validity

In the sciences and social sciences, the word "validity" is used in many ways, but the most significant insight about its meaning and importance is revealed through its etymological origin. *Valid* comes to us from the Latin word for *strong*. In research, an experiment, a test, a concept or a measurement is considered strong, or "valid," when it corresponds to reality, that is, *founded in reality* but also *applicable to reality*.

There are two types of validity that political scientists should be aware of: *external validity* and *internal validity*.

In the social sciences, external validity refers to the extent to which the conclusions from the research or experiments conducted can be

---

REALITY CHECK

Why do we need a census?

The Canadian government's 2011 decision to replace the mandatory long-form census with a non-mandatory short-form census was criticized from many quarters of the research community. For example, in June 2012, the University Affairs website reported the following:

> On the same day that national media were scrutinizing newly released data from the 2011 census, a panel of researchers at this year's Congress of the Humanities and Social Sciences renewed their call for a return of the mandatory long-form census. "Why do we still need a census? Let me count the ways," said Susan McDaniel, Canada Research Chair in Global Population and Life Course and a sociology professor at the University of Lethbridge. Dr McDaniel called into question the data collected from the 2011 voluntary household survey because of the survey's low response rate.
>
> More than 98 percent of Canadian households responded to the 2011 short-form census, a larger percentage than in 2006. But the response rate to the 2011 voluntary National Household Survey, which replaced the mandatory long-form census, was just 69.3 percent. It isn't known for certain who didn't respond, but McDaniel said it's likely the non-respondents included disadvantaged groups and the rich. "So we have a biased sample," she contended.[2]

used to generalize about certain segments of the population or transferred to other groups or populations. For example, the criticism levelled at the Conservative government in 2011 for replacing the mandatory long-form census with a non-mandatory short-form census was entirely about external validity. Researchers questioned how valid the conclusions might be when there was a diminished response rate from certain poorer segments of the population.

In conducting any statistical survey, external validity can be improved by taking steps such as the following:

⊚ Increasing the size of the population sample.
⊚ Randomizing the selection of the population being sampled.
⊚ Ensuring that the participants complete the survey and do not drop out of the process.
⊚ Providing a reasonable explanation for why he participants' responses are similar or different from one another.

Some of the concepts commonly associated with external validity include the following:

⊚ **Predictive validity**: the extent to which a test or measure can be relied upon to predict outcomes for certain populations and in specific situations.
⊚ **Generalization**: a general notion or proposition obtained by inference from particular cases.
⊚ **Threat to external validity**: an explanation by the person making a generalization of how their generalization might be wrong.
⊚ **Experimental validity**: the notion that valid conclusion cannot be drawn without sound and ethical research design.
⊚ **Face validity**: the idea that a test or experiment has validity when it *looks as if* it will measure what is says it will measure.
⊚ **Criterion validity**: the idea that a test or measure can be valid if it compares favourably with other tests and measures already known to be valid.
⊚ **Selection bias**: prejudices or preconceived notions on the part of those conducting the research that might unduly affect the objectivity of the research and the evidence from that research

In the case of the new Statistics Canada census, one can see why researchers were concerned that data captured by the short-form, non-mandatory questionnaire might result in a selection bias and thus reduce the predictive validity of the survey, as well as the quality of the generalizations that could be made from the census data.

Internal validity refers to *the quality and ethical standards used in designing the research or experiment.* The manner in which note-taking, recording, testing, experimenting, surveying, etc., are developed and conducted matters a great deal and can often have a direct effect on the quality and the reliability of the data. In fact, one often hears of ethical *standards* in reference to research. This is not only about honesty and integrity in conducting research, but also about the manner in which findings are communicated. More on the idea of ethics in research later.

Reliability and Validity

Students who understand the meaning of reliability and validity, as well as the connection between reliability and validity, are more likely to avoid the many pitfalls of research and more likely to be successful in their research. As we saw above, reliability and validity both determine how much confidence you, or the people who read or hear your arguments, can have in the quality of your research and factual evidence. Reliability in research refers to the confidence we and others can have in the factual evidence that has been collected. Validity in research has to do with the *methods* that were used and the *manner* in which the data was collected.

In matters of confidence in our empirical data, much depends on learning the principles and methods of research and applying them every time. Table 2.1 will help us identify the various aspects of research methodology and its application to research, writing, and debating in political science. This table depicts the connection between reliability and validity in research. Both concepts are linked to the confidence we can have in the data that has been collected and to our confidence that the conclusions we draw from the data are as free of error and of bias as humanly possible.

Table 2.1 ◉ Connection between Reliability and Validity

Reliability	Validity
◉ Outcomes are consistent and can be repeated	◉ Outcomes meet the objective(s)
◉ Proof /verification/support is found in past data and events	◉ Proof/verification/support is found in ability to predict future events
◉ Uses a limited number of objective variables	◉ Uses a broader number of diverse variables
◉ Judgment is minimized	◉ Judgment is integrated
◉ Bias is avoided	◉ Bias is acknowledged

The application of concepts such as reliability and validity can be quite complex, particularly in the hard sciences and certain branches of the social sciences such as psychological testing and statistics. What is important to keep in mind here is that research methodology does matter and that academics and students do need to question whether the data that forms the basis of an argument is reliable and valid. Reliability and validity are at the very heart of a **peer review**, which is a *process by which a written work is reviewed, evaluated, and critiqued by professional peers in the same field of research before it is published*. During a debate, one of the most effective ways of undermining an opponent's arguments is to attack the reliability of the evidence or the validity of the techniques used in collecting the evidence. And so having a colleague, a professor, or a fellow student review the writing and the arguments before a debate or before it is formally submitted for a grade or for publication is a good idea.

Evaluating Sources of Factual Evidence

All scientists, including political scientists, investigate and conduct research in order to prove that a piece of information is actually a fact. But not all sources of information or data are suited to the task. The blessing and the curse of the Internet, for example, is that it contains so much information about all topics related to human understanding that one must learn to sift what is reliable and valid from what is not. In very general terms then, how do we evaluate the quality of the source material for use in writing an essay?

There are many factors to consider when determining the quality of a research source, and looking at those factors as we do our research helps us address the issues or reliability and validity. These include

- intended audience and purpose of the source;
- authority, authorship, and expertise;
- timeliness and currency;
- relevance; and
- integrity, objectivity, and bias.

Intended Audience and Purpose of the Publication

In assessing the suitability of a source, a good way to start is by asking who the audience is and what the intended use of this particular item or publication is. "Publish" actually means to make something publicly known, and the resulting publication can include any number of forms of communication from books and articles to music and engravings. And so the intended audience for a publication may be a factor in deciding whether the publication is suited to your task or to proving your thesis. For instance, a publication designed to provide entertainment news or fashion news, such as *People* magazine or *Vogue*, is unlikely to be suitable for someone writing an essay on proportional representation and electoral reform. That may seem rather obvious, but the point is that knowing which audience a publication is designed for will improve your chances of finding suitable sources.

Some books, encyclopedias, websites, television programs, and so on, have a reputation for being reliable sources of information. Ask your professor or a librarian at any school or local library for their opinion on the reliability and validity of your sources.

But you might also be able to tell from the author's credentials as well as the publisher's reputation. Some publishers have a good reputation in a particular field of study. Consider if the writer or publisher has a possible bias that might affect the quality of the information. Are they trying to sway your vote or promote a product? For example, students writing on the environmental benefits of using biofuels in our motor vehicles soon discover that there are many publications written by science writers paid by the biofuels industry to promote that industry.

As well-intentioned as these sources may be, they cannot be considered objective.

1. What is the article or book intended to prove?
2. Is the article published in a *scholarly* journal where *peer review* is required before publication?
3. Is the article published in a magazine designed to entertain and appeal to a broad popular base such as *Time*, *Maclean's*, or *Newsweek*?
4. Is this based on research? And is this original research?
5. How is the material organized and presented? Is it logically written, well-organized, and well-supported?
6. How extensive is the bibliography? Are there many, few, or no sources?
7. What are the writer's credentials, and what are they for?
8. Where is the funding for the research coming from, and is that clearly stated?

Authorship and Expertise

What is a **subject matter expert (SME)**, and why does it matter? A SME is *a person or an institution that is recognized as an objective and reliable source of information and opinion on your topic.* A SME could be a university professor, a non-governmental organization (NGO), or a research institution. But it could also be a journalist, newspaper columnist, or blog writer who specializes in a particular subject. Check the SME's background. If you are not certain that the material you want to use was written by an objective and reliable expert, ask your professor or a librarian. Ask these questions:

1. What is this SME's education, experience, or background?
2. What is the SME's reputation? Have they been accused of plagiarism or of falsifying research?
3. How well-known is the SME? Do other SMEs use or cite this SME in their research?
4. Who is the SME paid by? Does this SME have some other vested interest in the subject area?
5. Is the author an authority on the topic? What is their publication history?

6. Who is funding the research or the publication?
7. Is there a reputable sponsoring or hosting organization such as a university or government organization?

Timeliness and Currency

Harold Wilson, a British prime minister in the 1960s and 1970s, is credited with saying that a week in politics is a long time. Indeed, this adage applies to political science and all the other social sciences as well because societies are in a constant state of change. What was true yesterday may not be true today, and what is true today may not be true tomorrow. This is especially true in the twenty-first century as we undergo a series of rapid social, economic, and political changes at the global level owing in part to developments in information technology. So, it is especially important when writing about current events that our sources be as current as possible. In fact, the very nature of the field of political science attracts news junkies and people who like to keep up with current events.

Of course, not all forms of political science research are time-sensitive, and some fields of study change more rapidly than others. The historical analysis of political events and some forms of comparative politics are examples of research and writing that may not be very time-sensitive. But when you are dealing with current events, as political scientists often do, certain questions can help you sort the best from the worst:

- ⊚ Was this source published recently?
- ⊚ If you are looking at a website or web article, when was it last updated?
- ⊚ How recent are the publications listed in the bibliography or reference list?
- ⊚ Do the external links work or are they dead links?
- ⊚ How rapidly is your field of study changing?

Relevance

Deciding what sources are relevant and what are not sounds simpler than it is. Establishing relevance becomes easier as we become familiar with the subject matter, the research being conducted, and the researchers and SMEs of the field. In a sense, there is no real way of avoiding the familiarization process; like a baptism of fire, you just have to go through it. However, students can get help with this aspect of the research by speaking to their professors, fellow students, and librarians. The following are some questions related to relevance:

⊚   Is the publication directly related to my topic?
⊚   Does it help fill in background knowledge?
⊚   Does this source support my thesis?
⊚   Can this information be used to address the preliminary essay questions I have developed in preparing my thesis?

Integrity, Objectivity, and Bias

One way that scientists and social scientists ensure the integrity of the research in an article or book on a particular topic is to require that it be peer-reviewed before it is published in an academic journal. That is a requirement of most reputable journals. As mentioned above, a peer review is a process by which unpublished writings are reviewed, evaluated, and critiqued by professional peers in a particular field of research before they are accepted for publication. One often hears of peer reviews in medicine and in scientific journals, but they are common in political science as well. In this way, the integrity and the quality of the research can be maintained. At the same time, new discoveries and scientific knowledge can be shared with others, and the cause of advancing human knowledge can be promoted.

Central to the integrity of the research is whether the research has been coloured by

⊚   emotions,
⊚   political concerns,
⊚   the source of the funding,
⊚   biases, or
⊚   prejudices.

We all have emotional connections, political concerns, biases, and prejudices; however, writers in the social sciences must constantly guard against inserting their personal biases and prejudices into the discussion. Political science essays are, after all, a scientific exercise in which the facts must be allowed to speak for themselves. As explained before about the differences between political science and hard sciences, political science writings often have a qualitative aspect because of the rapid and fluid nature of social change. The writers may sometimes speculate or make generalizations that rely a great deal more on probability than other sciences do, and those may not always be based fully on reality. The effects of change on the discipline of political science will be discussed later in this chapter.

As political science writers, we also have to give the impression that our opinion is founded on factual evidence and not influenced by emotions, political concerns, biases, and prejudices. More often than not, the impression of objectivity is as important as the act of being objective because the reader needs to believe that we are objective. For the sake of credibility, therefore, essay writers in the social sciences are discouraged from using first person pronouns (e.g., "I," "my"), or phrases like "in my opinion."

Some publications, websites, and news programs are well-known for having a bias. In Canadian journalism, some consider the *Toronto Star* to have a centre-left bias, the *Globe and Mail* is often considered to have a centre-right bias, and the *National Post* and *Calgary Herald* are considered to be slightly to the right of the *Globe and Mail*. This does not mean that the news coverage from those newspapers should be treated with suspicion; rather, it means that the reader will want to be aware of the publisher's ideological perspective and understand that such perspectives can influence what news is published and how news is interpreted and analyzed. One could balance the possibility of bias in news coverage by using more than one news source. Here are some integrity-related questions one might want to ask about our information sources:

◉ Does the information appear to be presented in an impartial tone, or is the author using emotional language?
◉ Does the author have an ulterior motive, such as trying to publicize an idea or product for personal gain?

◉   Does the writer or publisher or website host have a financial or political motive or some other conflict of interest? Who is funding the publication? Is the funding at arm's length, or does it depend on a specific point of view being promoted?

◉   Are any political, personal, or religious biases evident in the research and in the approach to the topic?

One way to avoid the accusation of being biased might be for writers to make allowances for the possibility that they themselves might have a bias and that their research and their writing may have been affected by their bias. For instance, writers may directly address the issue of bias by declaring what their bias is, or they might offer an explanation of what their bias might look like if they had one. A political scientist designing a voter survey during an election, for example, might want to avoid the possibility of *selection bias* by ensuring that the sample of the voters being surveyed is representative of the voter population. Moreover, the designers of the survey must be able to show what measures they have taken to avoid selection bias. Note the discussion above about internal validity.

Other Pitfalls to Be Aware Of

Simply being aware of the possibility that some sources of information might be tainted with bias or shoddy research can help political scientists to avoid some of the pitfalls of research. Two popular sources of information that political science students need to be especially wary of are the present-day news media and the Internet.

Evaluating the News

News is defined as *information about important or interesting recent event, especially when published or broadcast.* News can be anything from a movie star's family drama (*soft news*) to multilateral agreements on nuclear disarmament (*hard news*). Increasingly, news seems to be more concerned with the softer news and whether the news story is entertaining: hence the term "infotainment" rather than factual or sociopolitically important. In this so-called "Age of Information," the rapid pace of change is particularly evident in the nature of news coverage worldwide, and many academics and journalists see this as an issue of some social and political importance especially for liberal democracies. Even the most cursory review of the literature on this matter reveals a broad and general concern about the declining quality in the coverage of news, its socio-political implications and its effect on many fields of study, not just political science. *Dailysource.org*, a Florida based non-profit organization dedicated to providing high-quality news and information for the global community, lists several key features of this decline, including high levels of inaccuracies in reported news; mistakes that regularly don't get corrected; sensationalism; poor coverage of issues related to the environment, government, education, and foreign aid; higher-quality reporting in non-profit organizations than profit-driven organizations who see making profits as more important than serving the public; short attention span of the media and lack of in-depth reporting; and media consolidation (or concentration) in the hands of fewer owners.[3] For example, in the early 1990s, fewer than 17 per cent of newspapers in Canada were independently owned, and since then a number of large mergers have reduced that figure to less than 1 per cent.[4] A 2012 report called *Media Ownership and Convergence in Canada*, states:

> Of the eight media conglomerates listed here, three—Rogers, Bell and TELUS—are dominant players in the wireless market. Furthermore, these three companies, along with Shaw and Videotron, dominate the Internet market. The dominance by a small number of firms in these markets becomes a greater concern as the Internet becomes more important to Canadians, with a handful of firms having potential gatekeeping power over the content Canadians wish to access.[5]

With respect to journalistic integrity, Neil Henry, dean of the Berkeley Graduate School of Journalism, says the following about news coverage in the United States:

> The digital age is witnessing an evisceration of American newsrooms, and with it erosions in content and traditional journalistic

standards. But this crisis also presents challenges and opportunities for universities. For one thing, the university has long been a significant source of news and information for the press. With the collapse of our traditional systems of news, how will that information reach the public in the future, and in what form and quality?

In the absence of professional journalists specializing in health, for example, who will report news of the latest medical research to the broader public, and its implications for society? With ever fewer highly trained education and science reporters gainfully employed, who will cover the important policy and fiscal issues connected with those critical fields, and their intersections with government and society?[6]

How, then, do we evaluate the relevance and value of a news story in preparing our arguments and essays? The following questions could be used to evaluate the value and reliability of a news story:

1. What is the main purpose of the news story or report?
2. For whom is the news item intended?
3. What is the most important information in the article?
4. What are the concepts crucial to the understanding of the article?
5. What are the credentials or expertise of those reporting or of those being reported about? For example, how much confidence could you have in a piece on electoral fraud written by a reporter who is known for his or her sports reporting?
6. Is this item written by an **artificial grassroots organization**—an organization that seeks to influence public opinion and government policy in areas related to manufactured products, drugs and health products, media, real-estate development, agricultural products, etc.? Sharon Beder, a professor at the School of Humanities and Social Inquiry at the University of Wollongong in Australia, has written extensively on the way corporations create fake grassroots organizations (or pressure groups) to sway public opinion and overcome regulations or opposition to their activities.[7]

7. Who paid for the research or the survey being reported? Was the funding "arm's length," meaning not dependent on the research results?

Asking questions such as those is an essential part of any broad, general education and should be a matter of routine for any post-secondary student.

What has always fascinated me about political science is that it is a field of study that requires a multidisciplinary approach. In the field of international relations, for example, one needs to know about geography, ethics, human psychology, diplomacy, economics, warfare, and so on. That being said, the sheer complexity of this field can make it almost impossible to keep track of current events around the world. In his 2014 book, *The News: A User's Manual*, the philosopher Alain de Botton notes that the amount of news available today is almost limitless. He suggests that we "personalize" our news consumption so as not to be overwhelmed or distracted from what is important.

> We are now conscious that the supply of news is almost limitless; that every day yields an exabyte of images and words, and that newspapers and news bulletins are in truth thimblefuls of information pulled out of a boundless ocean of data by hard-pressed editors, daily forced to do no better than guess at the desires of a putative "average reader."
>
> Inevitably, they don't always get it right. They may go on too long about a West African war or an incomprehensible debt repayment scheme. They may update us against our will about a society wedding or a Caribbean hurricane. We may feel as if we were being force-fed entrees we never ordered.[8]

De Botton says that we can use the technology available to us through our computer to automatically sift through the day's news offerings and tailor these filters to suit our needs and our personalities. According to de Botton, there are six types of news and he explains how each type might define our personal reality.

Political News—News that that should "elicit our interest in the complex mechanics of our societies, help us agitate intelligently for their reform and accept certain obdurate limitations without fury. . . . It should monitor not just those in power but all the systemic ills that hold back the community, while additionally recognizing its own momentous capacity to influence the values of the nation in comments on."

World News—"This subspecialty should open our eyes to the nature of life in foreign countries over and above their moments of bloodthirsty and dramatic crisis. . . . It should, by appropriating some of the techniques of travel literature and by constant recourse to great photojournalism, help us humanize the Other, in our minds, shaking us out of our globalized provincialism."

Economic News—"Ideally, this genre should not only illuminate current economic developments but also investigate the many intelligent and workable theoretical approaches which could effect saner, more fulfilling versions of market capitalism, thereby quashing both our unnecessary cynicism and our immature rage."

Celebrity News—"In this category, we would be introduced to some of the most admirable people of our era—as judged by mature and subtle criteria and guided as to how we might draw inspiration ad advice from them."

Disaster News—"The tragedies of others should remind us how close we ourselves are to behaving in amoral, blinkered or violent ways."

Consumer News—"This field of journalism should alert us to how complicated it is, within an aggressively commercial society, to generate genuine happiness by spending money."[9]

Evaluating the Internet

The Internet is both a wonder and a worry. More and more students are using the Internet to do all of their research. And many of the concerns discussed above about the news media also apply to the Internet. The wonderful thing about the Internet is that it contains a universe of information readily available to those who want to use it. The worrisome thing about it is that it contains a universe of information readily available to those who want to use it. Sifting quality information from garbage on the Internet takes patience and skill. The printed material found in a library, for instance, has already been evaluated, screened, and catalogued by librarians and experts in various fields. Much of the work has already been done for us. But unless one goes to a website that also does this important work, there are a multitude of pitfalls to avoid. Care and a judicious application of critical-thinking skills are necessary whenever Internet research is involved. Here are a few pointers:

⊚ Have a clear idea of what you are looking for.
⊚ Decide with the help of your professor or a librarian, which search engines are suited to your topic.
⊚ Don't rely on web sources alone; use other sources such as books, articles, or documentaries.
⊚ As you do the research, keep track of where your information comes from (e.g., authors, publishers, dates, URLs, etc.)
⊚ Establish who the intended audience is and what the website and its contents were designed to do.
⊚ Determine who the author is and what the website affiliation is.
⊚ Establish when the content was written or uploaded.
⊚ Finally, as was said above, question the reliability and the validity of the information being provided.

You must evaluate websites you intend to use for research. Not all material on the Internet is good quality, and not all blogs contain first-rate information, because not all blogs are written by experts. As great a resource as a free and accessible website such as *Wikipedia* is when you want to find out something immediately, it must be taken with a grain of salt. Did you know that not all of the articles on *Wikipedia* are written by experts? While *Wikipedia*'s publishers have taken steps to improve the accuracy and integrity of the content by establishing editing criteria, it is still an open-source website and as long as the writer(s) meets the editing criteria, anyone can modify an entry. The "good article criteria" can be accessed at: http://en.wikipedia.org/wiki/Wikipedia:Good_article_criteria

However, it may be wise to remember that *Wikipedia* encourages contributions no matter who is writing the article, and while there are efforts to maintain the quality of the contributions, one can never be as certain whether a contribution has been vetted for accuracy and quality.

How You Can Contribute

Don't be afraid to edit—*anyone* can edit almost every page, and we are encouraged to **be bold**! Find something that can be improved and make it better—for example, spelling, grammar, rewriting for readability, adding content, or removing non-constructive edits. If you wish to add new facts, please try to provide references so they may be verified, or suggest them on the article's discussion page. Changes to controversial topics and Wikipedia's main pages should usually be discussed first. **Contributing to Wikipedia** will provide you with resources on all the basics needed to use, comment on, and contribute to Wikipedia.

Remember—you can't break Wikipedia; all edits can be reversed, fixed or improved later. Wikipedia is allowed to be imperfect. So go ahead, edit an article and help make Wikipedia the best information source on the Internet![10]

That quotation about editing entries in *Wikipedia* should make anyone wary of the validity and the reliability of the articles on the website. How then does one evaluate the validity and the reliability of the information on a website such as *Wikipedia*? It is very important when using an open-source website that you ask

1. What type of publisher or publication is this?
2. Was this published by a university, a trade or industry group, or an interest group?
3. Who is paying for this website?
4. Is the publication written to inform you or to persuade you to act, behave, or vote in a certain way or to buy something?

5. Can the information on the website be verified by other reliable sources?
6. Does the website name its sources and provide links or standard bibliographical references?

Although there are many free publications from world-famous scientific and medical journals, it is wise to be wary of the easily accessible and free things you find on the Internet; it may be worth exactly what you paid for it. De Botton offers us some instructions on how to control Google News manually by using the "Personalize your news" button on the right top corner of the Google News page and how to adjust the slider for how much you prefer the news from a particular section.[11]

Evaluating Statistics

Statistics is *the science of collecting and analyzing numerical data, especially in or for large quantities, and usually inferring proportions in a whole from proportions in a representative sample.* There are essentially three types of statistical methods or approaches:

⊚   *descriptive statistics*—seeks to describe what a set of statistical data is saying without using either inference or probability;
⊚   *inferential statistics*—seeks to reach conclusions that go beyond the simple interpretation of the statistical data; and
⊚   *predictive statistics*—seeks to draw predictive conclusions from statistical data.[12]

It is always fascinating to see how a statistic in a front-page headline will capture the imagination of the reader and be remembered and by those same readers as though all we needed to know was the statistic without understanding the origin or the context of that statistic, and whether that statistic is worthy of justified true belief. Without context and analysis, the statistic risks becoming a **factoid**: *an assumption or speculation that is reported or repeated so often that it becomes accepted as fact.* As the definition suggests, factoids take on a life of their own and are like unconnected dots in boundless space.

Students can avoid becoming the purveyors or the captive of statistical factoids by learning the meaning of terms such as *average, mode, median,* and *margin of error.* The questions below should be considered when trying to determine whether data is worthy of justified true belief:

1. What is the purpose of the statistics? Or what issue or concern prompted the research?
2. What are we being asked to believe, and are the claims or conclusions reliable?
3. What is the context?
4. Is this a descriptive, inferential, or predictive statistic?
5. What is the source of these statistics, and how valid and reliable are the numbers?
6. Is there a possibility of bias? Does someone stand to gain from this particular interpretation of the numbers?
7. Has all of the data been released, or has the data been vetted in any way?
8. How old are the statistics?
9. Is the theoretical approach being used to interpret the data effective?
10. Is the connection between the cause and the results clear or is it spurious?
11. What is the margin of error?

Again, the questions above are meant to encourage critical thinking about statistical data. Students can deepen their understanding of the creation and the interpretation of data by taking courses, reading books, and seeking professional help from those who have specialized in the topic.

Explaining Trends and Making Generalizations

A critical element of any published research is the manner in which the author chooses the important pieces of evidence, finds patterns, and makes generalizations about the findings. As explained in Chapter 1, a generalization is an inference that what is true for one or a few is true for all. Generalizations are very common in news and Internet media, for instance, where writers try to establish patterns of data that may be interesting or entertaining but may not be factual.

There are many pitfalls in making generalizations and drawing conclusions, particularly in political science because it may be difficult to pin down the beginning and end of a social phenomenon (such as globalization or trends in social media) and because social changes may occur as a result of factors that can cause quantitative and qualitative changes, including

- ◎ time,
- ◎ age,
- ◎ place, and
- ◎ size.

These factors, also known as variables, are ever-present and may sometimes cause social change to occur very quickly, which makes it difficult for anyone studying in the political science to stay *current*. Moreover, the evidence must be continually verified in order for findings to remain current. And explanations must also be expected to change or be very general to apply to many social phenomena. The constant state of change may be seen by some as the curse of political science and other social sciences; however, I have found that those who enjoy following politics enjoy staying current and don't see it as a waste of time and energy. Let's look at the variables in more detail to see how these might affect our understanding of society and our ability to generalize about society:

Time: In recognizing patterns in history, it may be difficult to pin down the beginning and end of a social phenomenon For example, when did Beatlemania begin? And when did it end? An educated guess is probably the best answer to these questions.

Another example of the influence of time on our daily lives can be found in sayings such as "Time stands still for no man or woman" or Harold Wilson's famous remark that "A week in politics is a very long time." Mr. Wilson's remark was likely the result of some event, scandal, or stray comment that completely changes the prospects of a politician's getting elected. So it is with society and with the social sciences; people change their minds, often overnight. What is in style today may quickly fall out of fashion. Consequently social scientists must constantly be aware of the variability of popular opinions and habits.

Place: What is true in one place may not be true in another. This is especially true in political science, where, for example, generalizations made about the system of government in one country do not always apply to that of another country. Comparative politics is both a branch of political science and an empirical research method designed to explain the similarities and differences between countries with respect to their domestic policies, political institutions, and international relations.

Age: One of the factors a social scientist must constantly be aware of is that a person's values, beliefs, and ideas about life, family, and society are likely to change with age. As the population ages, for example, economists can anticipate—but never be 100 per cent certain—that there will be changes to people's overall economic needs, such as housing, transportation, health care, and entertainment.

Size: Social phenomena are also subject to variability because of size. What happens in small groups may not be the same in larger populations. Richard Attenborough's comment that he had never seen a problem that wasn't easier to solve with fewer people certainly applies here.

One last point about data, that because society is constantly changing, data is forever in danger of being dated. Very much like food, some data has a more distant expiry date than others, and we must regularly clear out whatever has the potential to cause harm if swallowed.

Ethics in Research

Regardless of the kind of research one is doing, whether it is primary-source research, such as reading diaries or designing an experiment or a poll, or secondary-source research, such as surveying books, articles, or Internet publications on a topic, ethical standards need to be applied. In fact, for research to be considered scientific and for a piece of evidence to be considered factual and reasonably believable, one must be able to demonstrate that ethical standards were applied. Ethics is a complex matter, which varies significantly from one profession to another and from one field of study to another. However, certain qualities and concepts are associated with all forms of scientific research. The tenets of this code include the following:

Honesty: Students and academics should strive for honesty in all of their communications. This includes publications but also research findings, data, and research methods.

Care: Probably the most important determinant of the quality of any work is the attention to detail with which research, argumentation, or writing is done.

Objectivity: Research must be conducted with impartiality and without emotion, political motives, bias, or prejudice. The evidence must speak for itself.

Openness: Research needs to be conducted in an open manner so that every aspect can be reviewed and critiqued by others, including your peers, colleagues, professors, and other experts.

Integrity: The concept of integrity includes conduct with moral uprightness, honesty, soundness, and wholeness, and without corruption or impairment.

Respect for intellectual property: Notwithstanding the obvious issues of honesty and integrity, and of giving credit where credit is due, plagiarism and other breaches of this code also have a lot to do with preventing research and publications from being done expertly and professionally and for the advancement of human knowledge.

Social responsibility: This is an ethical concept that relates to the obligation to act for the common good and to promote social justice.

Respect for colleagues: Fellow students and colleagues should be treated considerately and courteously in all circumstances.

Competence: Research is expected to be performed accurately and efficiently and, under certain circumstances, with well-maintained qualifications.[13]

Ask a Librarian

By definition a librarian is someone who has been professionally trained to find information in all its many forms (in books, articles, databases, magazines, art, and audio recordings, on the Internet, and so on).

Libraries themselves are large collections of information, and they are designed to help their patrons obtain the information they need in the most straightforward manner possible. Both in public libraries and libraries attached to an educational institution, the librarians evaluate, collect, and organize material and try to make it as easy as possible for the library's users to find. By starting your research at your college or university library, you can be certain to find reliable material and librarians who are available to help you if you run into problems.

Another thing to keep in mind about libraries is that much of their collections are now available online. Online databases, e-books, and collections of streaming video make it easy to do some or all of your research anywhere, any time,[14] and most college and university libraries even have a service that allows students to talk to a librarian online. Librarians are vital resources for anyone looking to do research, and they can also answer your questions about how to document your sources (something that we will be discussing in more detail later). They can answer questions like these:

1. How can I find a journal article on this topic?
2. Is there a database that I can use to find primary sources?
3. What is a keyword or subject heading?
4. How do I know what database to use?
5. My searches are turning up too many resources. How can I narrow them down?
6. How can I tell if a journal is peer-reviewed?
7. I have the title of a journal. How do I access it?
8. I found an article listed in a database and it doesn't have full text. How do I get it?
9. How do I find something in print on topic *x*?
10. This library doesn't have the book I need. How can I get it?
11. How do I cite a CBC documentary or newscast?
12. How do I know my information is reliable?
13. Can I use citation management software to produce my works cited list?
14. How do I set up alerts so that I know if a new article is published on my topic?

15. How can I search for newspaper articles on a current event? On a historical event?[15]

In fact, the best way to make use of a librarian's expertise is to come up with a list of questions such as those above.

Identifying Keywords

Choosing keywords for research is an important skill since so much research is done through online or database searches. For a very useful worksheet developed by Seneca Libraries that helps you choose words that will be important in doing your research, preparing your argument, or writing your essay go online at oupcanada.com/Menard.[16] In addition, the worksheet will help you devise some important questions that need to be addressed by the research and keep track of your research sources for citation purposes.

The identification of keywords will be discussed in more detail in Chapter 4, which explores their importance to building strong arguments.

Annotated Bibliographies

Most students understand that a **bibliography** is a list of books and other works referred to in a scholarly work and printed as an appendix. An **annotated bibliography**, however, is a list of such works with a brief description or explanatory note about each one. Whether your professor asks you to make one or not, annotated bibliographies are a very practical way of keeping track of your research and your findings. They are an especially good place to start the thesis formulation and the writing process. Think of the annotations as the first paragraphs of your essay.

Some professors ask their students to begin the research for an essay by finding a number of articles, books, or video documentaries on the essay topic and writing a short description (usually one or two paragraphs) of them. The annotated bibliography may be titled "Works Cited." The annotated bibliography is essentially a list of works a student has found that will be used to write the essay, along with a brief summary of what each one contains. Here is an example of a citation with an annotation for an introductory textbook on Canadian politics as if one were doing and essay on the Canadian electoral system:

> Brooks, Stephen, and Marc Ménard, *Canadian Democracy: A Concise Introduction* (Toronto: Oxford University Press, 2013), Chapter 9.
>
> Chapter 9 of this introductory textbook contains many theoretical concepts and definitions as well as historical context that is essential for understanding the role that elections and political parties play in Canadian democracy. According to Brooks and Ménard, elections are perhaps the most important opportunity for most Canadians to participate in their political system. This chapter explores how Canadian citizens participate in their democracy and the nature of that participation.

Please note from this example that regardless of documentation format (MLA, APA, or Chicago Style), the citation should contain the four basic elements of a proper citation: the author, the name of the work (such as an article, book, documentary, podcast, or video), the publisher, and the date. In other words, all the information needed for the reader to find the source should be in the citation.

From the annotation, the professor can quickly see whether the student's research is achieving the desired goal, and the student begins the actual writing and thinking that are necessary for the essay to be successful in arguing its point. The student may also begin to see a pattern and develop ideas for how to formulate his or her arguments for a debate or an essay. In short, the annotated bibliography is likely to save time and energy, particularly if the student's research is heading in the wrong direction. Appendix 2 (posted at www.oupcanada.com/Menard) contains an Annotated Bibliography Worksheet that will help students collect essential information during the research phase of their project.

Conclusion

Some training in research methods is essential for any student of political science. This chapter explores a wide range of concepts associated with research methods. Two concepts that are vital to the quality of research are *reliability* and *validity*: both concepts have to do with establishing factual evidence and reasonable belief, and also with the manner in which the evidence was gathered. In addition we have examined ways of screening information and avoiding the many pitfalls in political science research. A proper grounding in research methods involves the application of scientific approaches to gathering and creating factual information. It also involves the application of critical thinking and ethical standards. Not only will those who read this chapter save time and energy in their studies, as well as improve the quality of their writing and the soundness of their arguments, but there should be a markedly less stress and frustration in finding suitable resources and writing the actual essay.

Review Exercises

1. Design a research schedule for a research assignment, allowing plenty of time for research, writing, and editing.

2. Name three key terms recently covered in class, and then find three definitions for each. Individually or in a group, compare the definitions and then choose the definition that works best for the topic.

3. Find a news story that uses one particular statistic or set of statistics as its starting point and, using the analytical tools explained above, determine whether the statistics are worthy of justified true belief.

   (Here is an example of a 2012 news story reported by the CBC that relies heavily on statistics: *Having young kids keeps Canadians from voting booth*, http://www.cbc.ca/news/politics/having-young-kids-keeps-canadians-from-voting-booth-1.1242688.)

4. Choose a topic and identify three key concepts that are directly connected to the topic. Define the term and, using a mind map to establish the connections between these concepts and your topic, formulate the questions that will need to be answered if you write about the topic, and establish what research you will need to do on the topic.

PART II

Writing

3 The Writing Process

Prose is architecture, not interior decorating.

—Ernest Hemingway

It seems safe to say that practically all forms of writing are argumentative to some extent. Whether the writing is **narrative**, a *written account of connected events in order of happening;* **expository**, *writing intended to explain or describe something;* or **descriptive**, *writing that serves as a description or seeks to describe without expressive judgment or feeling,* the author will directly or indirectly ask you to believe that his or her story or point of view is valid and true. Some writing, however, is more argumentative than others. That is particularly true of political and political science writing. Books, essays, and speeches in politics and political science are by their very nature argumentative and are designed to convince rather that entertain. The other significant difference between political writing and many other forms of writing is that political writing has a scientific underpinning. For this reason, this chapter discusses the basic principles and conventions generally taught to political science students.

For the purposes of this book, we will define **essay** as *a written composition on any subject.* That use of the word "essay" originated with Michel de Montaigne, a famous sixteenth-century French essay writer. *Essai* is French for "trial" or "attempt." What are political science writers trying or attempting to do? They are trying or attempting to prove a point, a thesis. They are also trying to convince others that their point is worthy of reasonable belief. Moreover, a political science essay and the research connected to it are meant to advance the cause of human knowledge as well as the quality of civilized life, as is the case with essays in all the natural and social sciences.

Writing an essay is an extremely complex task and, arguably, one of the highest forms of communication, one that takes years of study and practice to master. Figure 3.1 illustrates the many and varied elements of a political science essay.

Indeed, when it comes to essay writing and argumentation, the learning never ends: if you are going to write about politics or study political science, you as well accept the fact and embrace it.

In order for an essay to be considered suitable for political science purposes, you need to follow certain guidelines of argumentative communication and scientific methodology:

a.   The topic must be **debatable**—*questionable or subject to dispute* and with two sides: one pro—*for the proposition* and the other **con**, *against the proposition.*

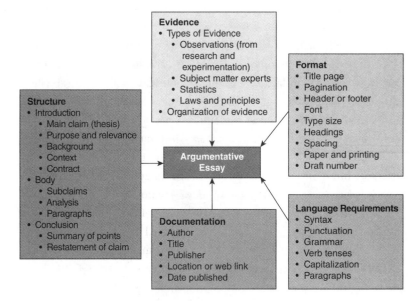

Figure 3.1 ◉ The Essay and Its Many Components

b. There must be a **proposition**—a statement of claim that is subject to proof or disproof.

c. The goal is to convince the reader or listener of the correctness of your proposition.

d. Established facts are not disputable. (e.g., That Canadian Confederation came into being on 1 July 1867: that is a fact and is not open to interpretation and debate).

e. The **premise**—*a previous statement or propositions from which another is inferred or follows as a conclusion*—must be built upon at least *three* main claims (See page 80 on the importance of the number three).

f. There must be evidence in support of your proposition.

g. There are two types of evidence: facts and opinions.

   Facts must be verifiable or capable of being proved. There are four kinds of facts:

   1. **Empirical observation**—facts based on observation or experiment and not on theory.

   2. **Natural law**—facts based on unchanging scientific principles common to the universe.

   3. **Statistics**—facts based on the science of collecting and analyzing numerical data.

   4. **Scientific measurement**—facts obtained according to the rules. Opinions are based on established expertise. (N.B. As a standard rule of thumb, unless you are an established expert [an SME] in the topic under discussion, your opinion does not count as evidence.)

h. Your purpose is not simply to inform, but to convince. As discussed below, how you present the argument matters. To that end, your first statements, that is, your **introduction**, is *the explanatory section at the beginning of a speech, documentary, essay, or book.* As we will see later, the introduction is very much like *a contract with the listener or reader.*

As can be seen from the guidelines above, what makes a political science essay different from, let's say, writing an essay on English literature, is its epistemological underpinning, that is, the scientific basis upon which the essay is built. However, before we discuss the basic elements of argumentation and how to integrate the scientific into the essay, we need to have a general overview of the structure of the essay.

Writing the Essay

There is something intimate about a good essay; one might even say that in the best essays, something like a conspiratorial bond is created between the reader and the writer. As Virginia Woolf wrote, "A good essay must have this permanent quality about it: it must draw its curtain round us, but it is a curtain that shuts us in not out." This bond is more about trusting that the writer can deliver the promised goods, and the bond of trust begins to be shaped in the first couple of paragraphs, that is, the introduction, or even in the first few lines. In order for the trust to be established, the writer will need to obey certain conventions of essay writing. A convention is a general agreement, custom, or customary practice, and the reader will want the writer to meet a wide range of conventions and expectations.

One of these expectations is that the essay be structured in the familiar and time-tested format of an essay. The typical essay, therefore, regardless of whether it is in political science or some other discipline such as English literature or the humanities, will have three parts: an introduction, a main section or body, and a conclusion.

Another expectation of the political science essay is that the scientific nature of the essay will be evident in the structure and the writing. Political scientists need to be able to demonstrate where the evidence comes from and how it was obtained.

The essay will need to include other structural elements and features such as these:

1. A **title**: Give your paper a title that clearly reflects the topic, your thesis, and what you plan to argue.
2. (Optional) A **title page** (not included in the page count) Provide the following information on your title page: type of assignment, title of essay, your full name, your student number, course number, course section, program, date, location, and name of course instructor.

3. An **introduction** including your **thesis** and a brief explanation of your purpose and how you plan to discuss your thesis. An introduction is an explanation of what the essay will argue. You may want to include some context and some historical background to situate the reader in terms of time and place. A list of the questions you plan to address may also be included. Overall, the reader should come away with some sense of what you want to argue and why this topic matters. Remember that *the introduction is a contract* with the reader and in order to fulfill the contract, you will need to meet certain expectations. An introduction can also be seen as a road map that tells readers where you plan to take them.

4. **Key terms and definitions** from your introduction, which should be used in your discussion to help the reader understand your arguments. As we will see later, definitions matter a lot, and the success of an entire debate can hinge on the meaning of a single word.

5. **Logical organization and sequence** using well-written paragraphs. A **paragraph** is *a distinct passage of text, dealing with the subject from one particular point of view.*

    Paragraphs are the basic units of the essay; they help the writer organize the evidence, explanations, and arguments in a way that is logical and persuasive. A basic rule of thumb about paragraphs is that there should be one paragraph for every new idea or twist on an idea.

    Another rule of thumb is that paragraphs should not be so long as to lose the reader's attention. A reader needs a certain amount of variety in order to remain concentrated on your argument, and long paragraphs may be too taxing for people who have limited attention spans. You may also consider *organizing paragraphs into sections by general themes.* Paragraphs are discussed in more detail below.

6. **Reference system** for your research using the documentation format required by your professor (e.g., MLA, APA, Chicago Style, etc.). Students are seldom experts in the field that they are writing about, therefore, they tend to use secondary sources and rely on subject matter experts (SMEs) for their evidence and data. The methods used in their research, as well as the results of their research, must be clearly on display for the readers to see. If you are asked by your professor, a fellow student, a debater, or a reader where or how

specific information was obtained, you must be prepared to show them immediately. For more information on research methods and the identification of suitable information sources, please refer to Chapters 1 and 2.

7. A **reference list** or **bibliography** listing the sources you used in writing the essay. Again, certain approved documentation styles will be recommended by your professor.

8. A **conclusion**, or a **closing paragraph**, which sums up your arguments.

One final but important aspect of essay writing that will help convince the readers and gain their trust, is to establish patterns. From reading the essay, the reader will need to see a pattern and, as in music, will expect that rhythm in the structure of the essay, the arguments, and the evidence. In writing the essay, therefore, you will the need to tell the reader what to expect (the introduction); tell them (the body of the essay containing the evidence); and tell them again (the conclusion). The reader will also expect a minimum of three pieces of evidence that support your thesis and your conclusion. This is why the most basic argumentative essay, as illustrated below, contains a minimum of five paragraphs: one introductory paragraph, three body paragraphs, and a closing paragraph. Let's discuss the importance of patterns in more detail.

REALITY CHECK

Time Management Tips for Writing Essays

How you organize your time for an assignment or a research essay or debate will depend a great deal on the nature and size of the assignment. However, here are a few tips:

1. Even if you have several months before the deadline, start now.
2. Once you have the assignment instructions and due dates, your first task should be to find a calendar and draft an essay-writing schedule that takes into account all of the phases of research and writing discussed in the Introduction. That includes time for identifying resources, reading the material, organizing the data,

continued

and most importantly, processing the information, and then actually writing followed by revising.

3. When you sit down to work, do so with a specific goal in mind.
4. Work in blocks of time, for example, 45- to 60-minute blocks.
5. Experts say that very little is accomplished beyond two hours without a break.
6. Take regular breaks—10 to 15 minutes every 45 to 60 minutes. That means getting some exercise or something to eat or drink.
7. Cramming is an inefficient use of time because it often results in unprocessed information and ideas, loss of focus, and a greater potential for errors.
8. Give your brain plenty of time to sort the information and make connections. Sleep is also essential to allow the brain to process information and work through difficult problems.
9. Separate the social from the homework. I know from bitter personal experience that I was more successful once I developed a daily study and writing routine. In fact, treating your studies as you would a nine-to-five job works remarkably well because it leaves most evenings and weekends for guilt-free rest and relaxation.

Lucky Number Three: Establishing a Pattern

It is generally accepted that one needs three instances or examples to establish a pattern. That is true in the sciences or in framing an argument or writing an essay. When writing an essay, you should strive to prove that there is a pattern, that the evidence, in at least three specific cases, can be linked to and prove the thesis. Unless a pattern has been clearly established in the evidence and in the essay structure, the reader may conclude that your thesis has not been proved. In essence, if there is no pattern, there is no conclusion to be drawn or argument to be made or written about.

Recall our discussion about reliability and validity in Chapter 2. If a scientific experiment produces the same result every time it is repeated, the experimenter can conclude that there is a reliable pattern and that we can confident in that fact. To use a hard-science example, if water at sea level boils every time it is heated to 100 degrees centigrade, then we can establish the pattern that water consistently boils at 100 degrees at

REALITY CHECK

Arguments, Essays, Paragraphs, and Hamburgers

Those who teach basic writing will often use the analogy of the hamburger to describe the structure of the essay and also of a paragraph. That is because, like a paragraph or an essay, a hamburger has three essential components: the fixings, which include or the hamburger patty, tomato, lettuce, etc. (the body of the essay containing the evidence), sandwiched between the top bun (the introduction), and the bottom bun (the conclusion). Together these three parts make a hamburger (an essay containing the whole argument). Apparently, this analogy works for most students.

Even the structure of a five-paragraph argumentative essay, the most basic of all argumentative essays, displays an absolute need to establish a pattern with at least three pieces of evidence and a simple rhythm.

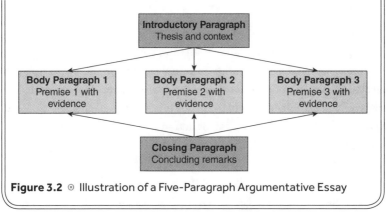

Figure 3.2 ⊚ Illustration of a Five-Paragraph Argumentative Essay

sea level. Anyone with the right equipment should be able to reproduce these findings.

A pattern suggests predictability. For example, political scientists and pollsters are constantly looking for patterns in demographics, such as in people's opinions by age group, region, gender, ethnicity, etc., in order to predict how voters will vote in an election. Voter behaviour in previous elections can not only point to patterns that can help predict electoral outcomes, but can also change government policy. In political science, a pattern may be evident in the responses of voters leaving a polling station on election day, or in the number of news reports on a particular topic. From the repetition in the responses (as with the boiling water experiment), we can assume that there is a pattern worth drawing conclusions about. Similarly, a pattern can be drawn from reading newspaper articles on a specific event or trend, and sampling opinions from various journalists may give us enough evidence from which to draw our conclusions.

Introductions as Contracts

Another important expectation from readers is that there will be an introductory paragraph or two that clearly set the tone and state the purpose of your argumentative essay. The introduction is probably the most important component of the essay. In a sense, the introduction is *the contract* you make with your reader. You are making a claim (your thesis), and you are promising to provide the reader with the factual evidence that supports that claim. Therefore, your introduction should, in some way, name the topic of the essay and outline the main points to be discussed. The introduction sets out the goals, scope, and tone of the essay. You will be judged on whether your mission has been accomplished and by what you said in the introduction that you would do. And it is such an important part of the essay that it is quite acceptable to rewrite the introduction after the rest of the essay has been written. Expect to write at least two or more drafts of the introduction.

Essay introductions come in many shapes and sizes. Some may be as short as one sentence, as is often seen in newspaper articles or essays by political columnists. Take, for example, columnist Rex Murphy's essay in the *National Post* "Universities have become factories for reinforcing opinion." In his single-sentence introduction, Mr Murphy makes it very clear what he thinks about Brandeis University's revocation of its invitation to the author and political activist Ayaan Hirsi to receive an honorary degree and to speak to their students:

> Brandeis University in Massachusetts showed itself to be gutless and pharisaical this week by revoking an invitation to

award the international advocate for women's rights under Islam, Ayaan Hirsi Ali, an honorary degree.[1]

Brevity is the essence of style, as they say, and in that one sentence, the reader can tell exactly what Mr Murphy is about to argue, and it's not about congratulating Brandeis University, and other universities like it, on their moral courage and rectitude.

Some introductions may be more than one paragraph in length, such as the one that begins this short essay by the economist Jim Stanford in the *Globe and Mail*. Stanford writes on the politics of the myth of Canada's strong economic recovery after the 2008 recession in "'That strong recovery? It was just a myth,'"

> Ever since the global meltdown of 2008, it's been an article of faith in Canadian economics that we somehow handled the whole mess better than the rest of the world. No banks collapsed. Our recession, while painful, was not nearly as bad as America's. Our deficits were smaller, and will disappear sooner. Not surprisingly, there's a strong political aspect to that smug mindset: Federal Conservatives never tire of claiming credit for this supposedly superior performance.
>
> The argument that Canada outperformed the rest of the world was overstated at the best of times. Even in the early years of recovery, several other countries (including Germany, South Korea, Australia) did much better at protecting employment and rebuilding incomes. But with the rest of the world now gaining serious economic momentum, Canada's boastful claims are increasingly far-fetched. Far from leading, we now lag other countries, and our relative underperformance is getting worse.[2]

Mr Stanford's first paragraph gives us the historical background and context, along with a very general sense of what this article will be about. And the second paragraph leaves no doubt that this essay will be a critical assessment of the Canadian government's "boastful" claims about the country's economic performance.

Also note Mr Stanford's use of "the rule of three" in the first paragraph as he tries to establish the general pattern of the Canadian public's beliefs about the nature of Canada's economy after 2008:

1. No banks collapsed.
2. Our recession, while painful, was not nearly as bad as that of the United States.
3. Our deficits were smaller and will disappear sooner.

In his first paragraph, Mr Stanford is saying the Canadian public had *three good reasons* to believe in the "myth" of Canada's economic recovery, but the next sentence of the same paragraph says that he may have evidence to the contrary.

So, as we have discussed above, a clear and persuasive introductory paragraph is the most important step in establishing a rapport with the reader and it opens the reader's mind to the possibility that your point of view may be worth listening to. The writer will then have to deliver on the promise of the introduction in the individual paragraphs found in the body of the essay. Those paragraphs are where the evidence, or the matter of the argument, is contained.

Paragraphs as the Basic Unit of the Essay

Mastering the art of essay writing first requires a mastery of paragraph writing. A **paragraph** is *a distinct passage of text, dealing with one particular point of the subject.* Paragraphs are the basic unit of the essay, and students will find essay writing much easier once they have a basic appreciation of its structure and developed the skill of writing a paragraph.

If the paragraph is the basic unit of the essay, the *sentence* is the basic unit of the paragraph. While some paragraphs may be as short as one sentence, political science students should strive to write paragraphs that are individual self-contained arguments. Like the essay, the typical paragraph has a three-part structure, containing three different types of sentences:

All paragraphs contain a **topic sentence**: a general statement that highlights and summarizes the main idea of that paragraph.

1. The **topic sentence** is the first sentence of every paragraph and tells the reader what the general idea or point of this paragraph will be.
2. The second sentence and subsequent sentences are known as **supporting sentences**, and their function is to *explain, expand upon, and support the topic sentence*. A supporting sentence can be a fact, a definition, an example, or a quotation. Every supporting sentence adds strength to the main idea of the paragraph or topic sentence.
3. The final sentence is the **closing** or **concluding sentence** that *summarizes and ties all of the ideas contained in the paragraph together*. The concluding sentence can be a reminder of what the main point if the paragraph was, or a restatement or paraphrasing of the topic sentence.

Keep the following pointers in mind as you write every paragraph: remember and focus on the main idea you would like to express; keep your topic, supporting, and concluding sentences clear and to the point; and finally, use a dictionary to make sure that the words you are using mean what you want them to mean.

Paragraphs allow the evidence you have in support of your argument to be grouped into separate and easily understood units. But how we organize these individual units in the essay is vital to the clarity and persuasiveness of the argument.

Organizing the Evidence and the Argument

Taking the time to organize the annotations discussed in Chapter 2 into a logical, easy-to-follow sequence will save time and energy and help to prevent frustration. The reader will also be thankful. The simple fact is that information becomes much easier to manage and to discuss with some kind of *predictable framework*. Ernest Hemingway's comment about architecture and writing seems most applicable here.

As with the building of a house, the architectural requirements of essay writing must be respected and the intended use by the owners—in this case, the writer and the reader—must be considered in the design. And that leads to a most important question about organizing the essay and the evidence: other than passing this course, what you are trying to achieve with this essay? What are you trying to prove and to whom? The answers to those questions will determine where to go from here.

One way of establishing the purpose more clearly is to ask about the organizational theme of the essay. Consider which of these organizational themes or types of classification apply to your essay by asking: Is this essay

◎ an explanation of cause and effect?
◎ a chronology?
◎ a comparison?
◎ an analogy?
◎ a series of examples?
◎ a set or series of illustrations?
◎ defining of terms and concepts?
◎ a classification?
◎ a description of a process?

For example, if your purpose is to discuss the historical development of a political phenomenon, perhaps a chronological approach to organization works best. On the other hand, if your purpose is to compare political systems, the essay may be organized along the essential features common to most political systems (e.g., the democratic institutions, the electoral system, or the judiciary) and the discussion will unfold along the lines of similarities and differences of those features. And again, if your purpose is to report the statistical findings of a survey, the essay may be organized in order of the most evident pattern of responses to the least evident.

Once these questions have been answered, you can further refine your choice of essay framework by looking at this classification of organizational types:

◎ Chronological order—time of historical occurrence
◎ Spatial order—organization on the basis of physical size or relationship
◎ Order of importance—organization on the basis of priorities or of least or greatest importance

⊚   Order of frequency—especially useful for discussing the results of an experiment or a survey

⊚   Topical order—organization based on the requirements of the topic itself[3]

In the case of topical order or order of importance, you could group several paragraphs by topic or importance into clear, separate sections and differentiate each section with a *heading* or a *subheading*. Headings and subheadings can help you organize the data, and more importantly, help the reader focus and interpret the data in a way that is helpful to your argument.

In any event, the manner in which your essay is organized will have a direct effect on how your evidence is received by the reader. There is no substitute for clear, logical thinking; your credibility and reputation will grow with the reader or the listener, and they will thank you by believing your assertions.

Transitions

How does a writer make it easy for the reader to follow the logic of his or her argument? One way is with the effective use of words or phrases known as transitions. **Transition words** are *commonly used words or phrases that establish a logical link between one idea and the next, between sentences, or between one paragraph and the next*. Transitions are words that help the reader make connections between the ideas and information contained in the essay or in an argument.

Table 3.1 shows there are many transitions. Which transitions you use in your writing will depend on what you are trying to achieve and the organizational theme of the essay: chronologically, topical order, frequency, and so on. For instance, if the writer is trying to compare two political systems, words or phrases such as "similarly," "likewise," "by comparison," "in the same way," "however," or "on the other hand" could be used. A chronological approach to organizing the essay may mean using a numerical sequence, and words and phrases such as "in the first place," "secondly," and "thirdly." Or another time-based set of transitions

Table 3.1 ⊚ Transition Words by Type and Purpose[4]

Type of Transition	Purpose	Examples of Transition Words	
Similarity or addition	Adds information that agrees with, reinforces, or contributes to a previous idea	likewise also furthermore as well similarly moreover in fact	next second again equally important indeed in the same way in addition
Contrast	Establishes an opposition between ideas; often leads to a conclusion or decision between these ideas	although despite conversely however even so instead even if though irrespective	whereas nevertheless while notwithstanding still on the contrary yet regardless rather on the one hand on the other hand
Sequence and causation	Establishes an order for ideas; shows how one idea follows from another	first thus second(ly) therefore third(ly) then consequently hence	subsequently next as a result before accordingly for this reason since because
Qualification	Adds a condition to the idea; sets limits or boundaries for the idea; considers possible opposition	for the most part sometimes generally granted often considering ordinarily	of course usually admittedly rarely unfortunately occasionally fortunately
Introduction	Brings an idea into the discussion	first(ly) with regard to to begin primarily in the first place similarly	initially regarding as for concerning in the case of when it comes to
Conclusion	Shows that the discussion of an idea is complete	finally to conclude ultimately in conclusion in the end in summary	in any case to sum up therefore without a doubt thus regardless

| Emphasis | Places more importance on the idea, drawing the reader's attention | notably in fact most significantly specifically primarily in particular | particularly most important(ly) above all essentially most of all certainly |
| Exemplification | Introduces an example of a previous idea | to illustrate take a look at for instance such as for example | one such example an example would be to demonstrate in one such case in this case |

might include words, and phrases such as "at that time," "in the past," "afterwards" and "since then."

The use of transition words is one of several ways to keep the reader's attention and maintain that all-important reasonable belief on the part of the reader. When paragraphs are somehow related or connected, and when every paragraph is in some way related to your thesis, your message becomes clearer and this adds to the reader's impression that the essay is well-organized, logical, and convincing.

Sentence Structure (Syntax), Grammar, and Spelling

Nothing destroys a writer's credibility more than faulty syntax, grammatical errors, and spelling mistakes. In fact, there is no point in writing an essay that cannot be understood because of such mistakes. Language errors force the reader to do extra work to figure out what is meant. You lose credibility because the errors distract the reader from the content and the argument, and suggest that there may also be mistakes of fact or logic in what you have written. Writers should endeavour to write sentences that are well-constructed and error-free sentences but also varied in structure and length so as to maintain the reader's interest. There are a myriad of books with instructions on how to write clear and error-free sentences and paragraphs: find one and use it regularly and religiously.

Document Requirements

Yet another expectation that readers have of a political science essay or book or blog, is that the actual document itself will have a certain look, contain specific elements, and follow a certain predictable format. An essay may be well-written and argued, but if the font, the spacing, or the manner of referencing sources is inappropriate, the writer will lose credibility. The document needs to look like a political science document.

What should the typical political science document look like? There may not be a definitive answer here and individual professors or publishers will have their preferences that are dependent on the reason for producing the document; however, for educational purposes, certain questions may apply:

⊚ Is it legible, free of language errors, and neat in appearance?
⊚ Is the document properly titled and the writer, recipient, and publisher or educational institution properly identified?
⊚ Are references clear, complete, and consistent throughout the document?
⊚ If this is an essay submitted for editing or comments, is there enough room for corrections and comments?

Moreover, the appearance of the documents may need to follow certain guidelines such as the ones listed below for a typical political science course:

⊚ The document must be word-processed and the length must meet the requirements of the assignment (page count does not include the title page or the bibliography).
⊚ Many professors and publishers prefer 12-point Times New Roman font.
⊚ Double spacing makes the document easier to read and leaves room for hand-written comments and corrections.
⊚ Leave margins of 1 to 1¼ inches on each side (approximately 2.5 to 4 centimetres) for comments and corrections. At the top and bottom, leave at least 1¼ inches where the page number and other

identifying information can be added, as well as comments by your instructor.

◉ Any theories, wording, facts, or statistics not your own must be acknowledged and properly referenced. Tell the reader which authorities or subject matter experts you used as you write your arguments. (See the section below on citing references)

As indicated above, guidelines may change from one social science or one course to the next, so it is best to ask your professor for his or her preferences before you begin writing.

Citing References and Plagiarism

First, it is important to remember that in academic disciplines such as the social sciences, it is all right to borrow other people's ideas, words, and research, but you must say where these ideas, words, and research came from. In fact, when in doubt, it is better to err on the side of caution and to over report rather than be suspected or accused of plagiarism: the trustworthiness of your research as well as your reputation as a student or as a professional could be on the line. In academic circles, for instance, plagiarism is a sin that is not easily forgiven or recovered from. That is why political scientists learn the art of citing and documentation, and follow very specific rules.

In the social sciences, there are some very practical reasons why acknowledging references in essays is a good idea and why plagiarism is a bad idea. **Plagiarism** involves *taking another person's ideas, invention, research, or property, and passing it off as one's own.* Plagiarism results in

◉ a theft of private property;
◉ a misrepresentation of your abilities and of your qualifications (In essence, you are not what you are pretending to be, and you may be misleading your fellow students, colleagues, or employer); and
◉ a weakening of the body of research in a given field of study.

Many professors, your peers, and society at large frown upon plagiarism for ethical reasons because it is theft, and stealing material or intellectual property is bad, not to mention unethical. But there are also very important practical reasons why plagiarism is bad. And this has to do with the very real and adverse social consequences of faulty research and weak writing.

This becomes clear when we consider that a society's quality of life, even life itself, can be jeopardized when research and writing are shoddy and knowledge is faked or falsified. There is the possibility that harm to others could come from scientific methods that lack integrity (that are not valid or reliable). This could include improperly sourced and referenced material because it makes it is difficult if not impossible to conduct a peer review of a study when the references are false or inaccurate. This is most evident in the medical sciences, where scientists and ethicists go to great lengths to ensure that research methods and standards are respected, because the consequences of doing otherwise can be calamitous or fatal for patients. Witness the August 2014 debate in the medical community over the use of untested vaccines and drugs for patients infected with the Ebola virus.

But the same is also true in the social sciences, where improper research, fraud, or plagiarism can result in faulty government policy, which may harm society. And in political science, as in other sciences, there is a requirement to "do no harm." Anyone interested in knowing more about the code of conduct should read the *Tri-Council Policy Statement: Ethical Conduct for Research Involving Humans*, December 2010.[5]

Whenever data is weakened by fraud, plagiarism, or a lack of proper understanding, the reliability and validity of the findings can be adversely affected and can cause harm. Some might liken the practice of fraud or plagiarism to flying an aircraft without understanding the navigational instruments, or building a house on a geological fault line. Both create uncertainty and danger. Even alleged cases of plagiarism can cast doubt on the policies and decisions made by the person concerned, not to mention damaging his or her career. In 2013 the director of the Toronto District School Board was forced to resign after being accused of having committed plagiarism in his doctoral thesis. Because this person was responsible for educational policies of a school board, one feels compelled to question every decision that this person was involved in.[6] If the ethical argument against plagiarizing does not sway you, then you might be swayed by the possibility of losing a job or your credentials. Any breach of trust, which plagiarism is, carries other repercussions. Even though the breach may not have been wilfully malicious, you will always be regarded with suspicion and you will have to prove over and over again that you are trustworthy.

One feature of human understanding is that the integrity of the research we are conducting today often depends greatly on the research that occurred yesterday. Think of it as a large pyramid of knowledge where the structure above, depends on the integrity of the structure below. How does a writer know the research they are using can be depended on if the previous research was faked or falsified? Acts of plagiarism may cause future research—the work that depended directly or indirectly on the work that came before it—to be flawed or false. If research is flawed or false, then the structures upon which we base our assumptions about life, society, or science may be weakened and unsafe.

Again, when in doubt, over-cite.

Referencing Basic Research Data

There are several citation formats, including MLA, APA, and Chicago Style. Social Scientists most often follow the APA or Chicago Style. However, what is most important for students to remember is that every citation needs to contain certain basic information that will make it easy for others to find the sources that you have based your arguments and conclusions on. Therefore, citations need to contain as much of the following information as possible:

⊚   author(s)
⊚   title
⊚   web publisher or print publisher
⊚   database
⊚   city where it was published (this could be very important, but it is not always required)
⊚   year when the work was published
⊚   if it is a website, the exact link
⊚   date the publication was accessed on the website
⊚   page numbers

As has been suggested several times, ask your professor or publisher for their documentation format preferences or guidelines. Librarians can also help. And, so as to avoid confusion in your reader, apply the guidelines judiciously and consistently throughout the essay.

Conclusion

Every time I sit down to write, I am reminded of the eighteenth-century writer and poet Alexander Pope, who wrote, "True wit is nature to advantage dress'd, / What oft was thought, but ne'er so well express'd." An essay may not be poetry, but it can be an art form. And in political science, essay writing is an art form with a scientific basis.

As with all essays, readers will have expectations. They will expect clarity and consistency. A political science essay is not a mystery novel, and readers will expect an introduction that clearly lays out what is to be argued and what lies ahead. They will expect that material will be organized into paragraphs, that there will be context, and that the ideas will flow well from one paragraph to the next. And remember that in political science there are conventions and expectations that relate to argumentation and to the scientific basis of that argument. Therefore, as the writer, you also have to convince the reader that your argument, or thesis, is worthy of reasonable belief from a scientific point of view. If the readers are to be convinced, they will expect clarity and consistency in the scientific methods of research, the references, and the documentation style. Here are a few final questions to consider when writing and editing your essay:

1. Does your essay have an introduction? What are you *arguing*? What is your *purpose* or *thesis*?
2. What made you choose this topic or theme? Whom are you writing for?
3. Have you defined your terms?
4. Have you made effective use of theoretical tools such as classifications, typologies, and taxonomies? (See Chapter 4 for explanations of those terms.)
5. Have you avoided logical fallacies? (See Chapter 4 for details on avoiding the pitfalls of argumentative writing.)

6. What is your *proof*? Do you have enough supporting facts (such as statistics, examples, or expert opinion) in each body paragraph to support your thesis? Remember that you need at least three of everything.

7. Is each body paragraph linked to the thesis?

8. What made you choose these *references* (books, articles, studies, or interviews) for your essay? What is each author arguing? How do these materials relate to your topic?

9. Have you cited your sources properly? Make it easy for the reader to find the sources you've cited. In fact, there should be absolutely no doubt where you got your data.

10. How are your research findings connected to your thesis?

11. Have you considered the possibility that you may be wrong? At some point in the essay (preferably near the end), you will want to let the reader know that you have been thorough in your analysis and that you have taken the other side of the argument into consideration. Don't be afraid of discussing briefly what potential critics might argue against your claim, and then explain to the reader how these counter-claims can be rebutted. In fact, if you expect to debate your thesis publicly, this exercise will be essential to your success.

12. Conclusion: what should the reader take away from the essay?

Therefore, your readers must be able to appreciate not only the beauty of your writing and the structure of your argument but also the scientific validity and the reliability of the evidence upon which you have built your argument. The importance of balancing the emotional appeal of the argument with the scientific basis of the argument will be examined further in the discussion of rhetoric and oral presentations in Chapter 5.

Review Exercises

1. Using the course calendar and assignment deadlines, write out a research and writing schedule.

2. Explain the difference between a fact and an opinion, and write an example for each.

3. Scan a publication for examples of empirical observation, natural law, statistics, and scientific evidence.
4. Identify a controversial current topic in Canadian society, such as euthanasia, legalization of marijuana, or taxation policy, and write a statement of claim that clearly reflects one side of the issue. Then, in two columns, list the arguments in support and the arguments against the statement of claim.
5. Take exercise 4 further. Pretend you have the task of writing an essay on the controversial topic, and write a one-paragraph introduction.

4 Preparing the Argument

Don't raise your voice, improve your argument.

—Bishop Desmond Tutu

Persuading someone to agree with your point of view is not the same as presenting them with a good argument. An argument can be persuasive because it appeals to the reader's or listener's emotions, to their ego, or to their prejudices; however, the same argument may not be worthy of *justified true belief*. Similarly, the ability to persuade is not as important to society as the ability to inform. In fact, history is replete with examples of effective political leaders and tyrants with appealing ideas who persuaded their people to act in ways that were not in the public interest. Another example can be found in the Sophists of Ancient Greece, who had a reputation as skilled rhetoricians. They had the ability both to persuade and to manipulate their listeners. John Poulakos, an expert in rhetoric at the University of Pittsburg who writes about Plato's view of the Sophists, suggests that not all of them used their skills in bad ways.

> Plato critiques the Sophists for privileging appearances over reality, making the weaker argument appear the stronger, preferring the pleasant over the good, favoring opinions over the truth and probability over certainty, and choosing rhetoric over philosophy. In recent times, this unflattering portrayal has been countered with a more sympathetic appraisal of the Sophists' status in antiquity as well as their ideas for modernity.[1]

The Sophists may have had training and ability in rhetoric, but if the people could be so easily manipulated by these morally deficient Sophists, it is because they lacked the ability, first, to recognize what was happening and, second, to make it difficult to be manipulated.

What if it were possible to be trained in the rhetorical skills of the Sophists but also in skills that encouraged the advancement of the common good? The good news is that there are a wide range of courses in the liberal arts, such as philosophy, the humanities, and the social sciences. The liberal arts are available to the general public in educational institutions across the country and are there to provide skills and meaning that go beyond technical knowledge. They are designed to teach the skills and techniques that prevent faulty reasoning and manipulation and promote the growth of knowledge for the greater good. We call these skills *critical-thinking skills*, and every discipline uses them in one way or another. It happens that liberal arts courses—courses that give the learner a broad, general education—tend to devote a large portion of the curriculum to the development of critical thinking.

Critical thinking is *the systematic evaluation or formulation of belief statements by rational standards*. The social value of teaching the general population critical-thinking skills is not only for those who make the arguments; it is also for those who listen to the arguments.

As the term "critical thinking" suggests, the thought process of the thinker involves critiquing the subject matter. In their quest for greater understanding, critical thinkers look at unclear thinking as well as unclear writing. In its simplest form, the critical thinking process can be as simple as asking the basic W5 questions: Who? What? When? Where? Why? But as most students can attest, the critical-thinking process for some academic disciplines can be quite complex and may take years of education and practice to develop.

Critical Thinking

In their pursuit of knowledge, or justified true belief, critical thinkers engage in one or more processes such as observation, experimentation, comparisons, reasoning, synthesis, analysis, reflection, and discussion, and so on. They will establish whether an argument is properly constructed and will actively seek, in a disciplined manner, to determine whether a statement or an argument is true or not. In order to achieve that, critical thinkers apply, together or in part, a set of skills, which involve the ability to infer, to analyze, to evaluate, to interpret, and to explain. One could argue that most of the courses students take, especially in the humanities and liberal arts (including political science), are designed to develop critical-thinking skills. And essay writing in political science is an exercise in critical thinking.

One way of looking at critical thinking might be to see it as a linear process that begins with some basic elements:

1. analyzing
2. problem solving
3. decision making
4. application
5. comprehension
6. evaluation

In fact, many instructors use a model, such as the one shown in Figure 4.1, that depicts critical thinking as a pyramidal-structure process that is somewhat linear in nature: "first we do this, then we do that." In a sense, critical thinking allows us to build our understanding as well as build an argument. This linear approach is valid and can be simple for most of us to apply and understand, and it may accurately describe what goes through a person's mind as he or she critically appraises a concept, look at data, or reads the daily newspaper.

That being said, using a linear or pyramidal approach to explain critical thinking may lead to an oversimplification of the process and miss the complexities and the many years of training that it takes to fully develop these skills. In fact, critical thinking processes can be extremely sophisticated and non-linear. As seen in Figure 4.2, perhaps a better way of describing and understanding critical thinking is to see it sometimes as *cyclical process* or sometimes as a *mind map*, with no fixed point of entry or point of exit. In other words, as the critical-thinking process may be linear, circular, or neither. In fact, in academic fields of study, the process never ends.

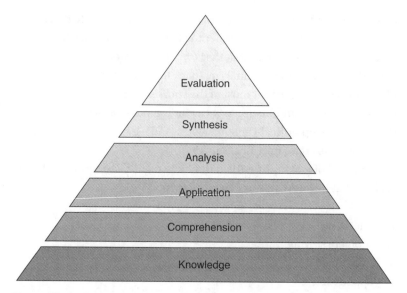

Figure 4.1 ⊙ Typical Depiction of Critical Thinking as a Linear Process Such as Building a Pyramid.

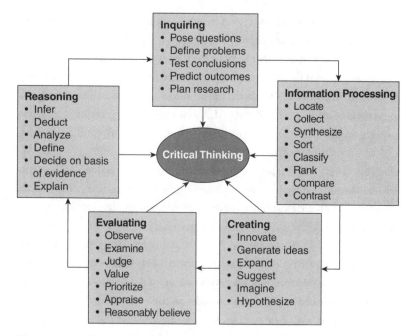

Figure 4.2 ⊙ Critical-Thinking Process: Actions and Skills

The National Council for Excellence in Critical Thinking (NCECT) is one of many organizations around the world dedicated to the advancement of critical thinking in societies. For the NCECT and organizations like it, critical thinking is a quality-of-life matter. The NCECT recognizes that certain *universal standards* must be met when critical thinking is involved; otherwise, justified true belief is not possible. Following are the seven universal standards:

⊙ *Clarity*—This is a fundamental requirement of any writing. An unclear statement leads to confusion, misinterpretation, and inevitably frustration.

⊙ *Accuracy*—You may be clear, but the argument is faulty if it is not accurate. When the facts are examined, will they stand up to scrutiny?

⊙ *Precision*—When we are precise, we tend to be both clear and accurate.

⊙ *Relevance*—Relevance has to do with focusing on the matter at hand and dealing with the matter directly.

⊙ *Depth*—The depth to which the research and analysis is conducted often improves the quality of the conclusions.

⊙ *Breadth*—In an argument, breadth refers to a person's ability to consider another point of view. In education, breadth refers to how broad-based a person's education is.

⊙ *Logic*—Logic refers to whether the facts and the argument are organized in a way that flows and makes sense to the listener or reader.[2]

It almost sounds as though these universal standards are the answer to countering the *seven deadly sins*. And in fact, the NCECT also lists seven *intellectual traits or qualities* that should be encouraged in the practice of critical thinking because they are qualities usually associated with persons of character and integrity: *humility, courage, empathy, integrity, perseverance, faith in reason,* and *fair-mindedness*. These are traits and qualities we are more likely to associate with heroic behaviour like that of war heroes, great political leadership, and parenting.

It would appear that once one has accepted the principles of critical thinking and the pursuit of justified true belief, a moral imperative and responsibility applies. If critical thinking unleashes the power of the mind, then once unleashed, what should be done with that power? As Uncle Ben tells Spider-Man, "With great power comes great responsibility." In any case, applying critical thinking skills means doing the work, trusting in the process, and travelling the road that the evidence puts you on. And the advancing of the argument, like promoting an unpopular government policy, passing a harsh sentence in a court of law, or making a difficult business decision, may mean hardship for the person in charge. Former US secretary of state, General Colin Powell's assertion about power and responsibility hints at what may be in store for those who have or take responsibility: "Being responsible sometimes means pissing people off."

A good argument persuades and has appeal because it is logical and worthy of acceptance, but the listener must first have some knowledge of what a sound argument looks like. How then do we recognize a good argument? Here are a few steps we can take.

Step 1—Establish the presence of an argument by looking for indicator words that denote the presence of either a conclusion or a premise in support of that conclusion.

Step 2—Examine the logic of the argument and determine whether it is a deductive or inductive argument. An argument is by nature deductive if we are being asked to believe that the conclusion is true because the premises are true. If the argument is not deductively valid and the writer is using terms such as "likely," "possible," and "probable," in relation to the conclusion, the argument is inductive. Assume that an argument is either deductive or inductive on the basis its form. (If it walks like a duck and talks like a duck, it must be a duck.)

Step 3—Examine the structure. For deductive arguments, if the argument is valid, check for soundness or the truthfulness of the premises.

For inductive reasoning, if the argument is strong, check for cogency or whether the premises are also true (or probable, likely, or possible).

Step 4—Examine the evidence. At this point, it can be assumed that the argument has not failed and is either valid or strong or both; we can proceed to an examination of the evidence.[3]

Let us look at each of these steps in greater detail.

Step 1: Establishing the Presence of an Argument: Indicator Words

The first step in assessing an argument is to *establish that an argument exists*. One can recognize the existence of an argument by looking for words that signal the presence of either a **premise**, *a statement or proposition put forth in support of a conclusion*; or a **conclusion**, *an inference from given premises or a judgment reached by reason*. (An **inference** is *the forming of a conclusion from premises*.)

As we read or listen we can recognize a premise by looking for words such as the following:

◎ because
◎ seeing that or given that
◎ since
◎ due to the fact
◎ the reason being
◎ inasmuch as

The presence of a conclusion is indicated by terms such as these:

◎ to conclude
◎ therefore
◎ thus
◎ we assume
◎ then
◎ it follows that
◎ hence
◎ which means that
◎ as a result
◎ so
◎ consequently

Here is an example with underlined indicator words (one line for words that indicated a premise, and two lines for ones that indicate a conclusion):

Because all whales are mammals [**Premise 1**],

and mammals are known to have kidneys [**Premise 2**],

<u>therefore,</u> <u>it is reasonable to believe</u> that all whales have kidneys.
[**Conclusion**]

Or

<u>Since</u> political scientists have been observed to be smart [**Premise 1**],
and Jack is a political scientist [**Premise 2**],
<u>we can assume</u> that Jack is also smart. [**Conclusion**]

Having established that an argument exists, we can move on to determining whether the argument is logical.

Step 2: Examine the Logic

The next step in assessing whether an argument is worthy of justified true belief is to *determine whether it is logical.* That means we must look at how the argument is structured and whether it is possible to believe it on the basis of whether the statements flow logically from one to the other. **Logic** is *the science of reasoning, proof, thinking, and inference.* Entire lifetimes and a myriad of books have been devoted to the study of logic. For our purposes, we will examine the quality of an argument on the basis of the following fundamental concepts: *consistency* (or reliability), *validity, completeness, cogency,* and *soundness.* More on this later.

Let's begin with a few examples of arguments and their structure. Here is a famous example of a logical deductive argument about Socrates:

All men are mortal. [**True Premise**]
Socrates is a man. [**True Premise**]
Therefore, Socrates is mortal. [**True Conclusion**]

In that case, the premises are true, and from these premises we can infer that the conclusion is also true. This three-part logical argument is also known as a *syllogism.*

But sometimes, the argument is not logical because neither the premises nor the conclusions are true:

All students are angels. [**False Premise**]
All angels have wings. [**False Premise**]
Therefore, all students have wings. [**False Conclusion**]

In the following example, both the premises are true, but something is clearly amiss because our own knowledge of the world we live in tells us that the conclusion is false:

All whales are mammals. [**True Premise**]
All humans are mammals. [**True Premise**]
Therefore, all men are whales. [**False Conclusion**]

Here the conclusion is not true. So then, even if each premise is true individually [humans and whales are both mammals], it does not follow that the conclusion is also true [humans and whales may share the characteristic of being mammals, but they are different species and not the same in all ways]. The argument here is considered invalid because there is *no logical connection* between the premises and the conclusion being offered.[4]

In instances such as this one, objective verification of the actual content of the argument may be required.

As we see here in this very basic discussion about arguments and logic, in order for an argument to work and to be reasonably believed, it must be logically valid and logically strong. A *sound* deductive argument, therefore, is one that gives you one or more good reasons to accept that it is true. More can be uncovered about the logic of an argument by delving into its structure and establishing whether the argument is *deductive* or *inductive* in nature.

Step 3: Check the Structure of an Argument

Having established that there is an argument and that the same argument is logical, we then proceed to an *examination of the nature of argument*. Arguments are based on two modes of reasoning: deductive and inductive. Once we've established the nature of the argument, we can judge the effectiveness and truthfulness of the argument with respect to the evidence that has been put forth in support of the conclusion.

Deductive reasoning is the *inferring of particular instances from a general law*. The basic logic of deduction is that if we believe the premises are true, then we can believe that the conclusion is true. Let's look at a couple of examples. In mathematics a deduction looks like this:

If A = B, and B = C, then A = C.

In political science, a deduction might look like this:

If an "Ontarian" is a citizen of Ontario, and Ontario is in Canada, then Ontarians are Canadian citizens.

Where are we most likely to see arguments of a deductive nature? We are likely to find deduction in mathematics, statistics, accounting, geometry, and the hard sciences.

The inverse of deductive reasoning is **inductive reasoning**, *the inferring of a particular law from specific instances*. Here are two examples:

Jill is a Manitoban. Manitobans are observed to be friendly (it even says that Manitoba is a friendly place on her automobile's licence plate). Therefore, we can assume that Jill is friendly.

French sociologist Émile Durkheim's statistical observations of Protestants and Catholics in the late 1800s led him to conclude that the Protestants had higher suicide rates than Catholics. And through induction, he was able to develop his now famous theories about religion, anomie, and suicide.

Where are political science students most likely to see or use inductive arguments? We use inductive reasoning to extrapolate, predict, or make a generalization about a whole population from a sample of that same population. Induction is used to make statistical generalizations, to make causal inferences, and to make arguments from examples. We make the inductive arguments in the study of international relations when we look at a country's past behaviour to anticipate or predict future behaviour.

Here again, there are indicator words that help us determine whether an argument is inductive or deductive. Indicators words or terms that signal the presence of a deductive argument look like this:

◉ certainly
◉ absolutely
◉ necessarily
◉ it logically or necessarily follows that

The presence of an inductive argument will be signalled by words such as

◉ probably
◉ likely
◉ chances are
◉ strong possibility that
◉ it is plausible

Note that when these words are used in an inductive argument, the result is a much softer in tone and certainty than those of a deductive argument. The softer tone is more likely to lead to further discussion and the possibility of a meeting of the minds, as well as conciliation and collaboration.

Good deductive arguments and inductive arguments are said to have specific qualities. Deductive arguments are said to be good if they are valid, truth-preserving, and sound. Let's look closer at what that means.

Valid—The term "valid" refers to the construction of the argument, and means that the argument provides decisive logical support for the conclusion. However, the validity of an argument does not mean that the argument is necessarily true.

Valid Argument:

All men are mortal. [**True**]
Socrates is a man. [**True**]
Therefore, Socrates is mortal. [**True**]

Valid Argument that is also untrue:

> All dogs are mortal. [**True**]
> Socrates is mortal. [**True**]
> Therefore, Socrates is a dog. [**False**]

Truth-preserving—In a deductive argument, the sense is that if the premises are true, the conclusion must also, and absolutely be true. Like food in a refrigerator, the truth in a good deductive argument, must be "preserved" in the conclusion. That is illustrated by the example of the Socrates syllogism.

Sound—An argument is *sound* when it is deductively valid and the premises are true.

> All mammals are warm-blooded. [**True**]
> Humans are mammals. [**True**]
> Therefore, all humans are warm-blooded. [**Also True**]

Inductive arguments are said to be good if they are strong and cogent.

Strong—In inductive reasoning, an argument is believed to be successful and *strong* when it provides *probable*, but not necessarily conclusive evidence. In these arguments, if the premises are true, then the conclusion is *probably* or *likely* true. The words "likely" and "probably" are often used in political science essays.

> Seventy per cent of the swans observed were white.
> Thirty per cent of the swans observed were black.
> Therefore, we can predict that the next swan we see will either be white or black.

Cogent—An inductive argument is said to be *cogent* when the premises are true. The swan example above is both strong and cogent because the premises are true.

Much of the work of political scientists is mostly inductive, and so we can expect that the critical analysis will centre on the strength and the cogency of an argument.

Step 4: Examining the Evidence

Once we have determined the nature of the argument, we can move on to the examination of the actual **claim**(s) made in that argument, that is, *a statement or assertion that something is true or false.* If the conclusion of an argument is to be believed, the claims made in the argument must be believable.

Arguments come in different shapes and sizes, and the following illustration shows us three different ways that claims can be put together in an essay to support your conclusion.

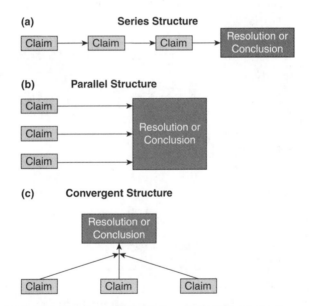

Figure 4.3 A–C ⊚ Structure of Claims Supporting Conclusions

All arguments are made up of claims based on evidence. If an argument is the simple justification of a claim using evidence, we need to look at what the audience is being asked to believe about the evidence and also how they are being asked to believe it. When a claim is made, the reader or listener is asked to accept the claim and the speaker or writer will actually give them a **warrant**: *permission, authorization or licence to make an inference and accept the claim.* Here is what a simple of argument looks like with the warrant:

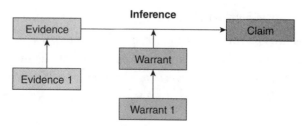

Figure 4.4 ◎ Argument with a Warrant

For instance, if the Canadian public is being asked to believe the government's claim that the economy is not in recession, the argument might look like this:

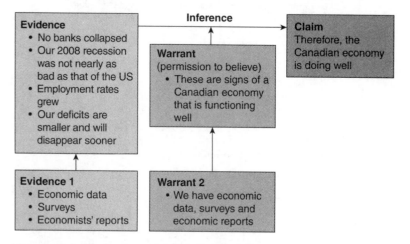

Figure 4.5 ◎ The Economy Is Not in Recession
Source: Adapted from David Zarefsky, *Argumentation: The Study of Effective Reasoning*, 2nd edn (Chantilly, VA: The Great Courses, 2005).

The use of the word "therefore" suggests that this is a deductive argument and that the reader or listener should accept the conclusion as one would a mathematical formula like $2 + 2 = 4$. The basis of this certainty is the evidence being provided for the claim that the economy is doing well on the basis of the economic data, the small deficits, and the economists' reports. One would think that this argument was a slam dunk, except for the fact that the individual pieces of evidence themselves are actually based on induction and need to be examined individually for validity and reliability before they can be reasonably believed. Until that is done, we could say that the claim has not yet been proved with absolute certainty. We could suggest that the speaker or listener use the term "it would appear," which denotes an inductive argument, rather than "therefore," which denotes a deductive argument. In fact, the conclusion may be found to be false if we uncover evidence to contradict it; that is precisely what the economist Jim Stanford was trying to do in his article "That Strong Recovery? It Was Just a Myth," which was discussed in Chapter 3. The quest for justified true belief in political matters never ends.

The rest of this chapter looks at other aspects of argumentation, such as defining one's terms, applying theoretical constructs, and fallacious argumentation.

Choose Your Words and Your Definitions Wisely

I often hear colleagues and other writers say, and have found it to be true in my own case, that unless you have put your argument in writing, you do not have an opinion worth discussing. It would appear that choosing the right word and a suitable definition is the first step in that direction. In fact, it can be argued that human understanding, knowledge, or comprehension is impossible without words and definitions. A word is the simplest and the smallest unit of communication and the basic building block of sentences. And with respect to words and argumentation, Voltaire once remarked that, without a proper **definition** (*a statement of the meaning of words or the nature of a thing*), a reasonable discussion is not possible.

That is true in essay writing and debating: establishing meaning should be your first objective. If you are not clear about the topic or the issues surrounding the topic, a good place to start is to look for and compare the definitions being used by different sides in the debate. In fact, some debates are entirely about each side's definition. For example, in a debate about whether euthanasia (medically assisted or voluntary suicide in cases of terminal illness) is desirable or acceptable, one side might choose to define euthanasia as "mercy killing," whereas the other side might define it as "murder." In such a debate, the debaters may never actually get beyond arguing over the definitions; that suggests that Voltaire knew a thing or two about arguments.

Word choice can have deep political implications. Take for example the way a writer might choose to use the words "kill" or "murder" to discuss a heated political conflict such as the Israeli–Palestinian conflict. To say that innocent civilians were "killed" in the conflict may evoke sadness, anger, or shock to be sure; but using the word "murder" in the same context may deepen the conflict because murder can be interpreted as being a judgment about legality, fairness, guilt, and morality.

Recently, a panel of six reporters—three from each side of the Israeli–Palestinian conflict—got together to identify and define words and their use in the media coverage of that conflict. The purpose of this dialogue was to find ways of reporting the news objectively by agreeing on words that were less inflammatory and less likely to evoke emotions and actions that might intensify the conflict. It turned out to be a very difficult task: of the 77 words that came up for discussion, the panelists could agree on only 21. Certainly, part of the difficulty in agreeing upon the meaning of a word is that it is used differently and with different connotation in different languages (e.g., English, Arabic, and Hebrew). For instance, as we see in the following box, the use and meaning of a word like *jihad* will differ greatly depending on whether the word is being used in the Arabic-language media, the Israeli media, or the English-language media.

REALITY CHECK

Dangerous Words

Few places in the world have a conflict that is as bitter and long-lasting as the Middle East, and particularly in the Israeli–Palestinian conflict nowhere is the language used to cover the conflict as subject to controversy. *Use with Care: A Reporter's Glossary of Loaded Language in the Israeli–Palestinian Conflict* was the product of a discussion about the use and definitions of words. The foreword contains the following remarks:

> The language that reporters use in covering this or any conflict can perpetuate stereotypes, can incite hatred or can simply deflect from more pressing issues. How this conflict

is covered is important, almost as important as what is covered.

For those reasons, IPI asked six journalists from the region to produce a guidebook for media professionals reporting on the Israeli–Palestinian conflict, which we hope will both promote dialogue and be of practical use.

Journalists should understand and choose their words in a way that is sensitive to the cultural and political realities of this long conflict, and we hope that this pocket-sized reference will help them to do so.[5]

The following table contains a few examples of those loaded words.

Expression	Explanation of Problematic or Sensitive Usage	Alternative
murdered נרצח (nir'tzakh) قتل (qutila)	Sometimes used by Israeli and Palestinian media in reference to any deadly attack on their own side, whether committed against a civilian or soldier/ militant, or by a civilian or soldier/ militant. *Murder* has a specific definition under the criminal codes of most countries, and therefore should be used with care. It is defined in the *Merriam-Webster* dictionary as "the crime of un-lawfully killing a person especially with malice aforethought."	assassinated / killed נהרג / חוסל (neherag / khu'sal) قتلأ غتيل (qutila / ughtila)
Jihad	This is a word that has different connotations for Israelis and Palestinians.	No alternative
ג'יהאד (jihad) الجهاد (al-jihad)	In Arabic and in Islam, the word *jihad* refers both to believers' internal struggle for piety, and to the external struggle against the enemies of Islam. Members of armed Islamist organizations, including groups that have been deemed terrorist organizations by Israel, the United States, and others, use the concept of *jihad* to justify violent attacks on civilians and to encourage self-sacrifice in the struggle against the enemies of Islam. As a result, Israelis understand *jihad* to mean terrorist activities in the name of Allah. Journalists should be aware of the meanings and connotations of this word for various audiences.	

continued

Expression	Explanation of Problematic or Sensitive Usage	Alternative
innocent civilian אזרח חף עמפש (ezrakh khaf mi-pesha) مدنيين ابرياء (madaniyin abriya')	Those killed or wounded in the conflict are sometimes referred to as *innocent civilians*. It is preferable to describe all victims or targets as civilians, omitting the prefix "innocent."	civilian אזרח (ezrakh) אזרח תמים (ezrakh tamim) مدني (madani)
aggression תוקפנות (tokfanut) عدوان ('udwan)	There is an Israeli view that this word is problematic when used as a blanket description for Israeli military operations, such as an air strike or broader military assault, because it immediately assigns blame; however, the Israel Defence Forces (IDF) might argue that the operation was carried out against a specific person who is involved in attacks against Israel, and who they, therefore, consider a legitimate target. For example: "Hamas condemned Israeli aggression in Gaza." Journalists should consider using the terms **strike / military operation** or **military assault**.	strike / military assault / military operation תקיפה (tkifa) מתקפה (mitkafa) غارة ضربة (ghara / darba)

Apartheid
 	
אפרטהייד
(apart-hayd)
 	
ابارتهايد
(abarthayd)
	Apartheid was the policy of racial segregation enforced in South Africa until 1994, through which the privileges of a white minority were entrenched at the expense of the black majority. It is understood to mean systematic government oppression on the basis of race.
	    Israeli activities in the Palestinian Territories are sometimes referred to by Palestinians and pro-Palestinians as acts of Apartheid, which is offensive to many Israelis because it implies that Israel has a clear and formal policy that regulates the superiority of one group over another. Israeli legislation punishes discrimination on the basis of race, nationality, or ethnicity, and Arab/Palestinian citizens of Israel have an equal right to vote and be elected.
	    Palestinians, on the other hand, argue that the comparison to Apartheid is applicable in connection to Israeli
		No alternative

	policies that enforce a separation between Israel and the West Bank, severely limiting the movement of Palestinians within the West Bank and into Israel.	
disputed areas במחלוקת אזורים (*ezorim be-makhloket*) ناز علي ها مناطق (*manatiq*) *mutanaza'* *'alayha*)	Some commentators or officials refer to **disputed areas** or **disputed territories**, which the United Nations and/or other international bodies regard as being under Israeli occupation, including the West Bank, East Jerusalem, and the Gaza Strip. There is technically a dispute, in that Israel does not accept these terms, but Palestinians and pro-Palestinians feel that reference to disputed areas legitimises the Israeli government's control of them.	West Bank / East Jerusalem / other specific geographical references (i.e., Use name of city or town). השטחים / הגדה / מזרח ירושלים (*ha-gada / mizra-kh yerushalayim / hashta'khim*) بيةلقلاشرقية، لقى فلقة غر مواقجغرافية (بلدانگسمثالـ (اسمامعينقلـموراك (*al-diffa al-gharbiya, al-Quds al-sharqiya, mawaqi' jughrafiya ['asma' lilmudun wal baldat]*)

Source: *Use with Care: A Reporter's Glossary of Loaded Language in the Israeli-Palestinian Conflict* - International Press Institute at http://ethicaljournalismnetwork.org/assets/docs/197/150/4d96ac5-55a3396.pdf. See the URL for more on this glossary.

The examples offer a concrete example of how difficult an agreement can become, but also how careful one must be in selecting words when defining terms or writing about or debating controversial topics.

Nothing can turn an audience against a writer or a speaker faster than the misuse of a word or the use of a word that generates unwarranted suspicions or hostile emotions. Here are a few guidelines that can help you with your choice and definition of words:

1. *Keep your thesis uppermost in mind as you select and define the terms.* Make sure there is a clear connection between the words or concepts, their definitions, and your thesis.

2. *Use a dictionary or encyclopedia.* A standard dictionary is satisfactory for most forms of writing, but if you are writing about politics, you may want to consider using a glossary, a dictionary, or an encyclopedia that specializes in your particular field of interest.

3. It may not be necessary to write your own definitions if you have done some research and have reliable sources. *It is all right to borrow words, concepts, and definitions from experts*; they have already done some of the work for you, and the audience or the experts won't mind, providing you have documented your sources properly.

4. In a debate or an argumentative essay, *make note of how your opponents or other writers use their words or terms.* Compare their usage and definitions with your own so that you are certain how your definitions differ from theirs.

REALITY CHECK

In order to make sure that you understand all sides of a controversial issue such as euthanasia, the legalization of marijuana, or the infringement of human rights by anti-terrorism legislation, use the table below to explain your position or the position of someone who might oppose your argument. Complete the following sentence about a potential opponent's position: "What my opponent is proposing is . . . ."

Legal and ethical	Ethical but illegal
Legal but unethical	Unethical and illegal

Then explain clearly how each of those four propositions fits or doesn't fit the argument being made. Conversely, complete this sentence: "My opponents would say that my proposition is . . ."
In a debate, one could ask the opponents to explain the legality or the ethics of their argument. Using such a tool may reduce the chance of misunderstandings.

Using Theories and Theoretical Tools

As the famous twentieth-century economist Frederick von Hayek said, "Without a theory, the facts cannot speak." What is a theory? A theory may be said to be *a mental conception or a scheme of thinking*, but simply put, a theory is *an explanation*. In the social sciences, a theory is an explanation of how a particular event or social phenomenon occurred. For example, economists may have a theory (an explanation) that the 2008 global recession was caused by the lending of money to first-time homeowners in the United States who could not afford to pay their mortgages in the long term. Economists may use this kind of theory to predict similar events in the future. For instance, an economist may have a hypothesis—*an assumption that needs to be tested against relevant evidence*—that in 2012, Canadians owed too much money, a situation which could lead to the kind of economic collapse seen in the United States.

To help us in our understanding of a particular social phenomenon, social scientists may use tables and charts, or even models, which are *theoretical and simplified (often visual) representations or description of reality*. As can be seen below, these visual representations make it easier for others to understand the connections between various parts, and for the writer to explain these connections.

Figure 4.6 shows David Easton's model of how the state works in any society. In this model, a country's political system is seen as a series of inputs—from a variety of citizens, interest groups, and

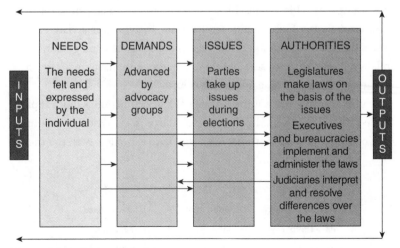

Figure 4.6 ⊚ Easton's Model

organizations—which then work their way through the institutions of the state for the benefit of society.

The term "paradigm," which has several meanings in the social sciences, can be useful to the political science essay writer in more than one way. First, a **paradigm** can mean *an example of something or a pattern of a phenomenon that we observe in society and can be used to identify a trend.* For example, "Company XYZ has developed a production model that has become a paradigm for how other companies structure their production."

Secondly, paradigm can mean *a way of looking at the world.* For example, the ideas of Albert Einstein and his theory of relativity (his paradigm) have given us a completely different way of looking at the universe.

And third, a paradigm can *be a way of looking at a phenomenon in order to explain it.* For example, Max Weber, the father of the social sciences, gave us a paradigm of the nation-state that is useful for explaining several social phenomena.

Other examples of useful tools and models we can use to explain political phenomenon are *classifications, typologies,* and *taxonomies.* Each one is designed to help the writer and the readers make, as well as understand, the connections between different sets of data. A **classification** is *a systematic distribution of information or material into categories.*

A **typology** is *a classification of characteristics or of human behaviour according to type.* In a typology, distinctions may be graded and ordered. The example in Table 4.1 classifies four different sovereign states, Canada, the United States, France, and Great Britain, by type. It is a visual representation of how each state has a different political arrangement, and makes it easier for us to see, and therefore understand, some of the basic differences between these political systems.

A **taxonomy** is yet another form of classification and is more sophisticated than a typology. Taxonomies organize information in a subject area and make connections between the data, as well as with the thesis.

Table 4.1 ⊛ Typology of Political Systems

Political System	Federation	Unitary State
Parliamentary	Canada	Great Britain
Republic	United States	France

But even taxonomies can be simple or complex. For example, Table 4.2 is Aristotle's attempt at explaining the differences between regimes and how a regime can be "good" or "bad". On the other hand, Lawson's taxonomy of political parties and ideologies, Table 4.3, is an example of a complex taxonomy with a greater capacity for explanation. It not only classifies political ideologies by type (right-wing and left-wing), but also offers connections that can explain significant differences between political parties (or movements), and each one's political beliefs and strategies.

Table 4.2 ⊚ Aristotle's Taxonomy of Good and Bad Forms of Government

	Rule on behalf of	
Who Rules?	**One or a Few (Bad Regimes)**	**The Many (Good Regimes)**
One-person rule	Tyrannies	Monarchies
Rule by a few	Oligarchies	Aristocracies
Rule by the many or the majority	Democracies	Polities

Table 4.3 ⊚ Taxonomy of Political Parties and Ideologies[6]

	Communism	**Socialism**	**Liberalism**	**Conservatism**	**Fascism**
Means of change	Revolution	Persuasion and democratic elections			Coup
View of human nature that influences how we interact with one other	Unselfish and social	Selfish and social			Selfish and unsocial
Role of the state	Economic redistribution	Protection of individual liberty and property			Control of society
Values	Economic equality	Freedom and political equality			Order
Position	Far left (Russian Bolsheviks of 1917)	Left (New Democratic Party of Canada)	Centre (Liberal Party of Canada)	Right (Conservative Party of Canada)	Far right (Fascists of the 1930s)

Any of the theoretical tools discussed above can make complex information easier to understand and to explain.

Explaining Cause and Effect

It may be useful to understand what is meant by dependent and independent variables if you are trying to explain the cause of a particular phenomenon. The term "variable" is both an adjective and a noun. As an adjective, "variable" means "changeable." But in the sciences, a **variable** is *a factor that can cause quantitative and qualitative changes.*

A **dependent variable** is the phenomenon we are trying to explain, and the **independent variable** is the factor that affects the dependent variable. The **intervening variables** are those factors that can influence both the dependent and independent variable.

Establishing patterns between variables is important in determining the existence of a natural law, i.e., a law that we can depend upon to make accurate predictions. In the hard sciences, for example, when the connection between two or more variables occurs regularly, like the effects of gravity on objects with a mass, scientists refer to this regular occurrence as a "law" (such as the law of gravity).

As was explained in the chapters on research, the existence of natural laws in the social sciences is unlikely because the sheer multitude of variables make it almost impossible to predict outcomes with the kind of certainty we see in the natural sciences. However, you might use variables to explain why many Canadians do not vote. The participation rate of eligible voters in the most recent Canadian general elections has been hovering around 60 per cent. You might hypothesize that the voting rates are connected to the variable of annual income and that the wealthier a citizen is, the more likely he or she is to vote. In order to prove this connection, you might look at whether the variable, wealth, is affecting the voting behaviour of Canadian citizens. The model in Figure 4.7 shows how the concept of variables is used to explain the social phenomenon of voter turnout. It connects the independent variable of income, which may be influenced by intervening variables such as education, knowledge, and ability to affect political outcomes, to voter turnout, which is important for democracy.

How voter participation is better for democracy

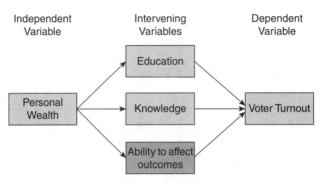

Figure 4.7 ⊚ Example of a Model

With this diagram, a written explanation of the factors that influence voter turnout will likely be much easier for a reader to understand.

Finally, how can a theory that has strong explanatory power be differentiated from one that does not?

1. State clearly what the theory is intended to explain, check it for consistency, and decide whether it can be relied upon to explain what it sets out to explain.
2. Check the evidence to endure that it actually supports the theory.
3. Compare the theory with other theories on the same topic.

In that way we can also determine whether the theory is valid and reliable. And finally, we can apply what Lewis Vaughn and Chris MacDonald call the *criteria of adequacy*, to help us judge the worthiness of a theory:

> **Testability:** *Establish whether there is a way or a test for determining whether the theory is true or false.* For instance, we can ask whether the theory actually predicts what it sets out to predict.
> **Fruitfulness:** A fruitful theory is one that helps us understand or predict something that other theories have not.
> **Scope:** A theory has scope when it explains the phenomena for which it was designed.

Simplicity: The notion that the fewer assumptions the theory makes, the better.

Conservatism: The theory conforms to our established beliefs.[7]

Arguments That Don't Work

As was noted above, arguments do not work when there is an error in reasoning and where the connection between the evidence that a claim (thesis) is not logical, non-existent or even false. The term for an argument that is not logical is "fallacy"; a **fallacy** is an *argument that is unsound by virtue of its rhetoric or logic*. It would be a mistake to think that fallacies have no appeal and are not persuasive. In fact, as the early Greeks noticed with the Sophists and sophistry, fallacies may have a psychological appeal to emotions, prejudices, and biases even though they are not logical.

The task of defining and of classifying fallacies can be complicated. One need only search for "fallacy" online to discover just how many fallacies have been identified and described by various authors, and even then, the list may be incomplete. Authors may name or categorize fallacies on the basis of their specialty, or they may choose to categorize fallacies according to type such as deductive fallacies, inductive fallacies, propositional fallacies, mathematical fallacies, fallacies of composition, and naturalistic fallacies, and so on. But for our purposes, we will attempt to group common fallacies into two kinds: fallacies with *irrelevant* premises and fallacies with *unacceptable* premises.[8]

Fallacies: Arguments with Irrelevant Premises

When the premises cited in support of a claim are improperly connected, the result is a fallacy with irrelevant connections. Somehow, the connection between the premises between the conclusion are weak or irrelevant.

a. A **fallacy of composition** occurs when the whole is assumed to have the same characteristics as one of its parts. The fallacy of composition is often made by persons making a generalization or a stereotype. Examples: *"I have met many Canadians; Canadians are so polite."* Or *"These politicians are corrupt; therefore, the whole Canadian political system is corrupt."*

b. **The fallacy of division** (the opposite of the fallacy of composition) assumes that what is true in one part is true in whole. Example: *"The House of Commons is dysfunctional; therefore, all politicians must be dysfunctional."*

c. The **appeal to majority** or **to popularity**: this kind of argument is often used by journalists, political activists, and populist politicians, who use the findings of surveys to support their writings or activities. For example, a person arguing for the legalization of the use of marijuana might write: "In 2013, the *Globe* and the *Star* newspapers reported that 67 per cent of Canadians polled supported the idea of legalizing marijuana. Therefore, we should legalize marijuana." The arguer goes on to suggest that if a majority of Canadians believe this, Parliament should legalize marijuana. This kind of argument is often used by populist politicians, that is, politicians who are concerned with the views of the average person. Ironically, populist politicians appeal to the common person when it suits their needs but accuse others of appealing to populist sentiments when it does not.

d. When the meaning of a key word changes in the middle of an argument, this is called **fallacy of equivocation**. Example: "To serve others is to act selfishly." Here, the word "serve" in the premise is somehow defined as a selfish act in the conclusion. There is no explanation for why the word "serve" should be defined as a selfish act. **Appeals to tradition**: Example: "We've always done it this way, it has worked in the past; therefore, it will work in the future."

e. **Appeal to emotion** or **to pity** occurs when the arguer tries to persuade the listener to agree with him by appealing to the listener's emotions. Example: "I am desperate: if you don't give me an A in this course, I won't be able graduate from my program, my parents will be very upset, and I won't be able to get a job." Here, the professor is being asked to give the student a higher grade, not because the student has met the course requirements but because to do otherwise would result in a personal calamity for the student.

f. When an argument appeals to ignorance or places an impossible burden of proof on the listener, the argument is known as a *nonfalsifiable hypothesis*, an *appeal to authority*, or a *conspiracy theory*. These arguments offer irrefutable proof like the word of an expert or authority, or even the word of God (in the Bible or the Koran), as evidence that their statement is true. In short, one is asked to believe as a matter of faith (in the authority of a holy person or a religious belief system) rather than as a matter of science, where the facts are established by specific rules and established methods. Example: "The Ten Commandments, given to us by God, say, 'Thou shalt not kill'; therefore, any killing is immoral and wrong." This statement suggests that no further inquiry or research is required because the expert or the authority says so and the authority is beyond reproach.

g.   **Genetic fallacy**: A claim is true or false because of who or where it comes from. Example: "Brian's argument about the Métis can't be true because he's not Métis."

h.   An **appeal to the person** (also called **ad hominem**) is made when we are asked to accepted or rejected a claim because of who is making the claim, rather than because the claim is true or not true. The ad hominem (Latin for "to the person") form of argumentation is often seen in political attack ads on television or YouTube. In the advertisement, the arguer might use a person's physical appearance or the way he or she speaks or dresses, and so on, as evidence that the person's political ideas, candidature for office, or policies are wrong. For example, in a 2008 video clip on YouTube, Stéphane Dion, the then leader of the Liberal Party of Canada *is seen with a puffin pooping on his head.* The caption that follows is: "Stéphane Dion is not a leader." Presumably, Mr Dion, no matter what his actual personal qualities are or what his proposed political policies are, cannot be leader because an animated cartoon has pooped on his shoulder. As ridiculous as it sounds, ad hominem fallacies and attack ads can have a significant impact during an election, especially if certain segments of the population already have doubts about the person's effectiveness as a leader or if the citizens are not well-informed about the election issues.

i.   The **straw-man** fallacy is an argument that misrepresents an opponent's position, and then attacks the misrepresentation instead of the opponent's actual argument. The straw figure (a life-size replica of a person meant to be blamed, is made of straw and set on fire) or beaten by an unruly mob of demonstrators. The straw figure usually represents a specific individual (often an unpopular political figure or an alleged criminal) who is considered by the mob, rightly or wrongly, to be entirely responsible for or guilty of some offence or calamity. The straw man is much easier to blame and kill than the real one, but for the technique to work, the audience must be relatively uninformed.

Fallacies: Arguments with Unacceptable Premises

Fallacies sometimes occur when we are asked to believe an argument where the application of the rules of logic has failed. A relationship exists between the premises and conclusion (unlike arguments with irrelevant premises), but there is something wrong with the premises that makes them unacceptable. Here are examples of what might be called unacceptable premises.

a. A **false analogy** is an argument that proposes that one phenomenon is exactly like the other. Example: "What happened at Ipperwash was exactly what happened at Wounded Knee." That statement suggests that the killing of an Aboriginal protestor at Ipperwash, Ontario, occurred under the same circumstances as the killings of protestors at Wounded Knee, South Dakota, in 1973. There is no proof here that this is a fact.

   Another example of a false analogy would be to state that civilizations are like biological organisms because they are born, they grow, they depend on institutions that are like body organs, and they deteriorate and die. However, on closer inspection, one may find that civilizations are not entirely biological in nature.

b. **Hasty generalizations** occur when the sample from which the generalization occurs is inadequate for the conclusion we are being asked to believe. Example: "We shouldn't vote for the Liberals in this election. The last time they were in office they introduced the GST."

c. The **a fortiori fallacy** is an example of faulty generalization. *A fortiori* means "all the more" or "with even stronger reason" in Latin. The author proposes that the more we have of something, the better will be the outcome. The following example is one we've heard a lot of since the 9/11 terrorist attacks in the United States: "The more security measures we have to combat terrorism, the more our freedoms will be protected." The *a fortiori* argument also presupposes that if one thing is true then it can be inferred that a second thing is even more certainly true.

d.   A **tautology**, or **circular reasoning**, says the same thing more than once. The author of such a fallacy tries to explain a phenomenon by using the same premises as the conclusion or the same phenomenon as the explanation. We often hear circular reasoning in sports reporting, as in *"A man's got to do what a man's got to do"* or *"It is what it is."* Another example of circular reasoning can be found in this statement: *"Armed conflict in Spain caused a bloody civil war in 1936."*

e.   Another form of circular reasoning is called **begging the question**. This occurs when the claim itself is already included in the premise. For example, "We should believe in God because the gospel says we should, and we should believe in the gospel because God said we should believe in the gospel."

f.   The **two-wrongs-make-a-right** argument is one where a morally wrong action can only be countered by a wrong of equal value. The "eye for an eye, tooth for a tooth" argument is often used by those who advocate tougher jail sentences for criminals; it suggests that retribution is the only good way of dealing with crime without much thought for the causes of the crime and for the consequences of the retribution.

g.   **False dilemma**: When the argument suggests, incorrectly, that there are few options available this is known as a false dilemma. For example, "In life, there are either friends or enemies, so, you should either love people or hate them."

h.   Arguing that doing one thing will have dire consequences or eventually lead to an absurd outcome is called the **slippery-slope** argument. Those who argue against legalizing drugs may sometimes use the slippery-slope argument: *"Marijuana is known as a 'gateway' drug; if we legalize marijuana, people will start using harder drugs like crack cocaine."* While the first premise may be true and the conclusion may be true, they are unconnected and the contention that one thing leads to another is false.

i.   The ***post hoc ergo propter hoc*** argument suggests that a phenomenon caused another phenomenon just because the first phenomenon occurred before the second. Example: *"The 2005 sponsorship scandal caused the Liberals to lose the federal election in 2006."* We are asked to assume that there is a connection between one phenomenon and the other. The case for the connection is never made.[9]

Classifying fallacies is a complicated business indeed. I have attempted here, in a very rough way, to categorize common fallacies into fallacies with *irrelevant* premises and fallacies with *unacceptable* premises. The reader should keep in mind that the number and types of fallacies can be dependent on the particular field of study.

Conclusion

Most citizens and consumers, and not only political science students, would do well to develop their critical-thinking skills and to be aware of sophistry and fallacies for the simple reason that corporations, parents, companies, interest groups, colleagues, politicians, and other people in authority knowingly or unknowingly use faulty reasoning and fallacies to persuade people to vote for them or to buy their products. It seems reasonable to believe that the ability to recognize fallacies—and be able to do it by type—could be an important step to refuting bad arguments. Critical thinking is a way for societies to protect themselves against manipulation and faulty decisions.

Steps in Judging an Argument

By way of reviewing what has been written above and of developing techniques for critiquing arguments and constructing strong ones, here are some steps that could be followed.

Step 1—Establish the presence of the argument.

Step 2—Determine whether this is a deductive or an inductive argument on the basis of indicator words.

Step 3—Examine the structure. For deductive arguments, if the argument is valid, check for soundness or the truthfulness of the premises. For inductive reasoning, if the argument is strong, check for cogency or whether the premises are also true (or probable, likely, or possible).

Step 4—If the argument has failed because it is not valid or not strong, proceed to the examination of the evidence.

In the social sciences, arguments are very often inductive, and therefore to determine the strength of an argument will require an examination of the premises to determine whether they are true. At the academic level, this may involve a peer review. At the undergraduate level, it may involve checking the research methodology, data analysis, and evaluation.

In a debate, as we will see in Chapter 5, many of the steps we have described here for determining the validity, soundness, and cogency of an argument are also effective strategies for attacking an opponent's premises and conclusions.

Review Exercises

1. Use a taxonomy to explain the differences between Canadian and American democracy.
2. As we saw in the article "Use with Care: A Reporter's Glossary of Loaded Language in the Israeli–Palestinian Conflict," the panel could not come to an agreement on certain terms. What were those terms? And why do you suppose the panel could not agree? Find other conflict zones and discuss these questions with respect to loaded language in those areas.
3. Classify regimes around the world according to Aristotle's classification of good and bad regimes, and using the criteria of the classification, explain what makes them so.
4. Look for commercial or political advertising in the media, and determine whether the arguments being used to persuade the intended audience are factual or fallacious. Name the fallacies.

PART III

Debating

5 The Art of Debating in Politics

In all debates, let truth be thy aim, not victory, or an unjust interest.

William Penn (1644–1718)

Chapter 4 began a discussion of how to develop critical reasoning skills, how to develop an argument, and how to recognize a good argument. Another way of developing our critical-thinking and communication skills is by learning the art of debating. The aim of debating in politics and political science is similar to that of writing essays in that we give our audience reasons to believe a claim. One difference, of course, is that the debate occurs in an open forum with an oral rather than a written delivery. Another difference is that the methods of communicating and persuading in a debate are both verbal and non-verbal. Successful debaters have an ability to harness a broad range of critical-thinking and communication skills that go beyond the written word. In fact, the non-verbal aspect of the oral delivery in a debate may as important as the verbal to winning that debate.

What is a **debate**? In its simplest form, a debate is *a discussion about a proposal or a claim*. By that definition, almost any discussion can be considered a debate; we have them around the family dinner table or between friends having a beer. However, in its highest and most complex form, a debate can be a formal and ritualized form of human communication designed to persuade others: those whom you are debating and those who are listening.

Why are we likely to debate? The purposes of debating are many: to influence outcomes related to a person, family, business or society, decide government policy, pass laws, advance human understanding, and so on. In fact, one way of testing the strength and validity of your argument is to debate your thesis publicly with someone who has prepared an argument on the opposite side of the same issue, and let the audience be the judge.

Where are we most likely to debate? Debates can be long, formal, and ritualized events, but shorter and effective debating exercises take place in classrooms across the nation.

In a classroom or debating society, debates can be part of a contest in which two opposing sides try to score points against each other before a panel of judges in order to win the argument. We can see broadcast debates on television or on radio such as on the CBC comedy program *The Debaters* or TVO's *The Agenda*. Formal public debates are held regularly in legislative assemblies, boardrooms, municipal council meetings, and courts of law.

What are we most likely to debate? Debate topics in political science seem to fall into one of two very broad categories: matters related to the allocation of resources, for example water and property rights, property use and development, budgetary allocations and expenditures, and so on; or matters having to do with values. As was pointed out in our introduction, values are most often related to our beliefs—such as beliefs in what is important or not important, ethical or not ethical, a priority or not a priority. Some of the most well-known and controversial values issues debated in Canadian politics have been the death penalty, euthanasia, equal rights, legalization of drugs, and abortion. It would be a mistake to believe that these issues are closed once a piece of legislation has been passed or the Supreme Court has announced a decision. One need only glance at a newspaper, news blog, or news broadcast to see that these debates live on in the collective consciousness.

Public Speaking and Oratory

Debates often involve public speaking; in fact, **public speaking**, or **oratory**, is defined as *the art or practice of formal speaking in public.*

Public speaking has many purposes: it is used to inform, to present, to entertain, to persuade, to explain, to influence, to announce, to celebrate, and also to debate.

What do great orators have in common? Recorded history suggests that the theory and techniques of oration (rhetoric) were first analyzed and discussed by the ancient Greek philosophers and Sophists some 3,000 years ago. The Romans themselves used this knowledge to train their lawyers and politicians. And these techniques have come through the ages and into our educational programs today. In fact, great orators are remembered across the ages and across cultures. We remember famous Greek and Roman orators such as Demosthenes, Cicero, Pericles, and Mark Anthony. More modern versions of noted orators include politicians such as Abraham Lincoln, Winston Churchill, Franklyn D. Roosevelt, Malcolm X, Christopher Hitchens, Margaret Thatcher, and Barrack Obama. They also include the more infamous versions such as Adolf Hitler and Benito Mussolini, whose speeches swayed entire nations though not always to desirable political action.

The basic principles of public speaking do not appear to change over time, and they seem unlikely to change without some significant technical innovation or radical genetic modification to our species. In fact, Aristotle's treatise on rhetoric and the art of persuasion, which was written in the fourth century BCE, is still in use in today's classrooms. Great orators either have training or an innate appreciation of what it takes to change people's behaviour and move them to action. In *The Art of Rhetoric*, Aristotle identified three modes of persuasion: the orator can persuade by means that are persuasive because of

a.   the character of the speaker,
b.   the emotional state of the listener, or
c.   the argument (or the logic) itself.[1]

Good orators are likely to use these techniques individually or combination as they try to win over their audience.

Many books, websites, and organizations devoted to the art of public speaking offer free advice on how to achieve the status of a great orator. Many concentrate on aspects of style rather than substance. And while there is no denying that image or appearance is important in persuading an audience to agree with your argument, it would be a mistake to think that appearances are everything. To use an analogy from the television cooking show MasterChef Canada, it would be like judging a dish by how it looks rather than how it tastes. In judging the quality of a speech and the argument being made, appearances do matter, but so does content.

If in our speeches and debates, we become too concerned with style and appearance rather than substance, we risk falling into the category of argumentation called **sophistry**, that is, *the use of intentionally deceptive or specious arguments or reasoning.*

Conversely, those who focus mostly on the facts and the logic of an argument and fail to appreciate the style of their delivery may fail to win over the audience because of their lack of personal appeal. The audience can sense when someone lacks *empathy*—that is the feeling the audience gets that the speaker really does understand them and what they need.

Aristotle's analysis of rhetoric helps us remember that the speaker's use of his or her personality and appearance is but one of three methods of persuading the audience. In the following list Aristotle's three modes of persuasion are used to classify the many characteristics of a good public speaker that are found on websites that offer public-speaking advice:

a. persuasiveness due to the character of the speaker
   - personality
   - passion
   - clothing—dress the part
   - vulnerability—evokes empathy and makes people feel that you are open, willing to share and not defensive
   - authenticity
   - sense of humour
   - fearlessness
   - expressive voice
   - plain speaking
b. persuasiveness due to the emotional state of the listener
   - empathy—knowing what the audience needs and showing them that you care about their needs

- knowing the audience's style of learning—verbal, visual, or conceptual
- make connections by telling a story—everyone loves a good story
- balance
- generosity (in a debate, being gracious to your opponents)

c. persuasiveness due to the argument (or the logic) itself
- good idea
- well-organized
- rational
- makes connections between the evidence, the claims, and the thesis
- factual
- well-researched
- properly sourced
- to the point
- topical

What we could conclude from that classification is just how complex the art of persuasion can be. Effective oratory takes a lot more work and preparation than many websites on this topic admit. In fact the Greeks believed that only the most *virtuous* persons could be a successful orator. In today's parlance, virtuousness is associated with moral rectitude and chasteness, but the Greeks used the term "virtuous" to refer to a person who had mastered the techniques of any fine art such as painting or playing an instrument.

Now that you have been introduced to the notion that there are different types of persuasion and the importance of substance as well as style, we need to discuss the theory behind the art of public speaking: rhetoric.

Rhetoric

As we have seen before, **rhetoric** is the art of effective or persuasive speaking or writing. In its most basic form, rhetoric has two main elements: **composition**, the act of putting together or constructing the message; and **delivery**—the manner with which something is said. In short, rhetoric deals with both the style of delivery and the substance of what is said. Aristotle says there are three genres or types, of rhetoric, and that which genre a speech belongs to depends on the reason for making the speech:

◉ *Deliberative rhetoric*—discourse most often of a political nature used to deliberate and weigh alternatives before a decision or a vote on a matter concerning the present or future
◉ *Forensic or judicial rhetoric*—discourse on past matters or actions such as those seen in a court of law
◉ *Epideictic or ceremonial rhetoric*—discourse used to praise or to blame and at ceremonies such as anniversaries, galas, commemorations, and state visits.[2]

Of these three genres of rhetoric, politicians and political scientists are most likely to use *deliberative rhetoric*. Deliberative rhetoric is seen in university and college lectures, at conferences, and in panel discussions. It is found in board rooms and in legislative assemblies of all levels of government across the country. The public will also see deliberative rhetoric during the public speeches and debates of election campaigns. We are literally surrounded with deliberative rhetoric every day.

Students of rhetoric are trained in what is commonly referred to as the *five canons of rhetoric*. The following five canons (categories) offer a theoretical approach to preparing for a speech or debate, but also a way of critiquing speeches and debates.

Invention—in rhetoric, invention means "finding something to say." That is where our earlier discussions about the *phases of research* and *choosing a topic* to write or speak about are most relevant. How does one invent a topic? By using what the Greeks called "*topics of invention,*" which in many ways refers to the type of analysis one might carry out on a particular topic, such as these:

◉ Cause and effect (for example, in a political historical analysis, examining how the American Revolution affected the British North American colonies)

- Comparisons (for example, in a comparative analysis, exploring Canadian democracy by comparing it to American democracy)
- Examination of relations (for example, in the study of international relations, a discussion about Canada's relations with the United States and their effect on Canada's relations with other countries)

In each of those examples, the *topics of invention* suggest possible approaches to "finding something to say."

Arrangement—a canon of rhetoric related to how a speech or written composition is organized. Rhetoricians might consider the following arrangement for an essay or speech:

- *Introduction*—As suggested before, perhaps the most important paragraph of a speech or essay because it tells the listener or reader what you plan to argue, why, and how. This is your contract with the listener.
- *Statement of facts*—Refers to the background and context that the audience needs in order to be ready to listen to the argument.
- *Division*—The concept of division is also known as the *partition*. It refers to the reason the speech is being made, and it separates each point that will be made in the argument as well as setting out how each will be discussed. In a debate, the division helps the speaker differentiate his or her approach from the opponent's approach. The division helps the listeners understand question such as these: What is the speech about, and should we be using deliberative, forensic, or ceremonial rhetoric? Who is giving the speech or writing the essay? And who is the audience?
- *Proof*—The part of a speech that sets out why we should believe the thesis. According to the Greeks, there are two kinds of proof:
  - **Intrinsic proof**: *proof used in the argument that is inherent in the object or subject*, such as definitions, named parts, species or characteristics, comparisons, and so on. Much of this proof, according to Aristotle, was invented by the person making the argument in the sense that that is who gives value to the proof in his or her argument.

- **Extrinsic proof**: *proof that is not invented by the person making the argument, but is used in support of the thesis.* That includes, statistical data, historical facts, documents, testimonials, legislation, and so on.

⊚ *Refutation*—that part of the argument where the person making the argument anticipates or refutes opposing points of view.

⊚ *Conclusion*—the summation of the argument.[3]

Style is the artistry with which the ideas are expressed. Style does not just refer to a superficial "look," but is about the way in which language is used in the speech or essay. That being said, style is both about an appeal to human emotions and the way in which the speaker establishes his or her credentials and authority to make the rhetoric believable. Rhetoricians speak of four stylistic groupings of oration:

1. *Virtues of style*—The virtues of style have to do with the quality with which one speaks and using a manner of speaking that is consistent with general norms such as syntax, vocabulary, pronunciation, and so on. There are five significant areas of concerns here:
   - *Grammar*—correct and acceptable language structure.
   - *Audience*—language suited to the audience one is speaking to.
   - *Effective and affective appeals*—effective debaters depend on facts and logic to get their point across; affective debaters use strong emotional phrases and deliver them with style and empathy for what the audience will respond to.
   - *Guiding principles of decorum*—Decorum refers to the behaviour of the speaker befitting the current situation in which the audience finds themselves; and there needs to be an appropriate balance between the ethical, social, and aesthetic properties of a speech. Two basic principles of decorum are aptness (suitability to the circumstances) and moderation (avoiding extremes of conduct).
   - *Ornamentation of language*—In rhetoric, ornamentation can be classified into two types:
     1. *Figures of speech or thought*—a form of rhetorical expression, such as metaphor or hyperbole, giving variety or force to the

argument. In rhetoric, figures of speech are the use of language such that the appearance of something happening is more important than something actually happening. For example, having a "lead foot" means to be slow; it does not mean having feet made of lead (although one could imagine an object made with lead feet.)

2.   *Tropes*—A rhetorical device consisting of a word or phrase. For example, "This place is a zoo." Or "He is an ogre." Or "This is a red letter day."

2.   **Levels of Style**—The level of style depends on whether the purpose of the rhetoric is deliberative, judicial, or ceremonial.

3.   **Qualities of Style**—a way of critiquing a speech relating to levels of style and qualities of style.

4.   **Figures of Speech**—Whenever we use words in a way that conveys meaning beyond the literal meaning of the words. Figures of speech are often referred to as ornamentation and by the way the ideas have been configured in language (See above for the three types of figures of speech.) There are many kinds of figures of speech. Here are a few:

- Pun
- Hyperbole
- Metaphor
- Euphemism
- Irony
- Personification
- Oxymoron
- Onomatopoeia
- Simile
- Understatement

With respect to figures of speech, it is probably a good idea to avoid clichés and mixed metaphors.

Memory—One aspect of delivering a speech is to memorize the material so that the speech can be presented effectively and with ease. However, this canon of rhetoric is especially important to public speaking during a debate or a public presentation where questions from the opposition and the audience are likely. This aspect of memory has to do with the ability to immediately remember and use what one has memorized to *improvise* when necessary. To use as cliché, we might also refer to the memory aspect of debating as the ability to "think on one's feet," and thinking on one's feet is not possible unless you, to use another cliché, "know your stuff."

Delivery—A rhetorical canon is concerned with *how something is said* rather than what is being said. These include techniques such as

a. *Voice*—the manner of style and expression that the speaker uses to convey the message. It goes without saying that a clear, confident voice (not too loud or too soft) makes a good impression, but it is wise to vary the intensity at appropriate times.

b. *Tone*—Tone is another way of conveying emotion and your attitude about your argument and the arguments of your opponents. How you have written your speech, your choice of words, and the structure of the argument will convey the tone. Tone can also reveal a bias about the topic.

c. *Hand gestures*—Hand gestures can be an excellent way of emphasizing certain elements of the speech. We use emphatic gestures most often in everyday conversations to stress certain points; by doing the same thing in a speech, you can make it sound as if you are having a one-to-one conversation with the audience and convey the sense of a regular conversation.

d. *Body language*—Much of the communication with the audience is non-verbal and comes from body language. Looking comfortable, at ease, and natural conveys confidence in one's ideas. If the body language expresses nervousness or does not express the tone correctly, the audience may intuitively question whether the body language matches the spoken words.

e. *Eye Contact*—To make eye contact with the audience is to connect with the audience. The audience will get the sense that you are speaking directly and personally to them. Even when reading from a prepared speech, it is a good idea to look up and make eye contact. It is also a good idea to look from one person to another.

f. *Dress*—The audience, or society at large, has a sense of what it is to be appropriately dressed. In fact the audience may find it difficult to get past the clothing style and into the details of your argument if you are wearing clothing that is unsuitable or that fails to show respect for the occasion. Wearing a T-shirt to deliver a eulogy or a wedding speech is simply "rude, crude and socially unacceptable."[4]

The five canons offer us not only the techniques for developing our speaking and writing but also a framework for critiquing essays and speeches. The five canons are entirely congruent with what was said about argumentation in the first four chapters of this book. And it may be useful to repeat that the ancients considered there were three ways of becoming a good public speaker: the first was to be *born with the innate ability* or talent to speak publicly, the second was to *learn the theory or art* of rhetoric, and the third was to *learn through practice*. But even if you were born with the innate ability of a great orator, the ability is useless without the theory, the training, and practice in developing that talent; in other words, education does matter.

Learning about rhetorical theory is certainly helpful for any student, but there is perhaps no better way to learn rhetorical techniques than by reading or listening to those who have mastered the art. One cannot help but be impressed by the wide range of techniques and the creative ways in which these techniques are used in persuading the audience (visit the companion site at www.oxfordcanada/menard for many fine examples).

Debating and Debating Strategies

Even though debates can occur in private between family members, business associates, email writers, or bloggers, we most often use the term "debate" to mean a public, structured contest between two or more debaters. Political debates are frequent during elections; examples of political debates can be seen in colleges and universities in an all-candidates' debates between representatives of each political party.

What follows is a discussion of how to prepare for a debate, sample debate formats, and tips for ensuring a successful debate. Success here is not defined by winning or losing, but by the quality of the discussion during and after the debate. These are desirable outcomes in the quest for human knowledge. In fact, the most successful debates are often those where the quality of the arguments by both teams is so high that there is no clear winner, and the audience is either undecided or evenly divided.

REALITY CHECK

Five Things to Know about Free Speech and the Limits of Free Speech

The attack on the French satirical magazine *Charlie Hebdo* (a publication that made the point of mocking religions) on 7 January 2015 by two terrorists raised the issue of whether there should be limits to freedom of speech even in a liberal democracy. For political scientists, this raises the question of what the average citizen in a liberal democracy should be allowed to say. According to Micheal Vonn of the BC Civil Liberties Association, there are five things every citizen should remember about free speech:

a. *Arguing against someone is not censorship.* This is a point that was made earlier in this book when I said that argumentation should be seen as a means of learning from one another and improving our quality of life, rather than as something to be avoided. Charter rights and some laws are sometimes used to silence opponents, and this kind of "Charter chill," or rights that one citizen holds against another, may actually be harmful to society in the long run.

b. *You should not face opposition.* Freedom of expression can also mean telling someone to "shut up." This is known as the *heckler's veto.*

c. *You don't take your rights everywhere you go.* You can say things in public places that you may not be able to say in private places. For example, you cannot make a public speech in the food court at your local shopping centre without permission from the owners. Vonn suggests that citizens need to be aware of what is a public space and what is not.

continued

d. *The state needs to protect more than one public good.* Free speech does not trump all other rights. For example, we have the right of privacy. Canadian courts have recognized that there needs to be a buffer zone around abortion clinics where protestors are prevented from interfering with something that is considered to be a private matter.

e. *Free speech is hard.* It requires an emotional and intellectual sophistication that we do not find in totalitarian regimes. *Charlie Hebdo's* satirical cartoons are considered by some to be an example of dreadful things that are allowed under the guise of free speech. For others, satire and the ability to shock are considered essential tools of positive social change. Arriving at a balance between what is allowable and what should be banned is "humanly difficult." We safeguard rights that you as an individual afford or grant to other individuals as you interact with them—a concept that is grounded in human dignity and is something we need to protect if we believe that a pluralistic society leads to a prosperous and more civilized society. Diversity is a strength and free speech protects diversity.[5]

Debate Preparation Guidelines and Strategies

The quality of a debate is entirely dependent on the quality of your preparation. The following is a set of instructions that will, if followed, improve the quality of the debate:

1. **Do the work!** A good argument takes time—for research, organization, and strategy. Previous chapters have already provided comments, instructions on research methods. Research and some thought will be needed to acquire the evidence to prove or disprove the resolution. But it is just as important to gain an understanding of your audience and to determine what appeals to them. Use the five canons of rhetoric to develop the argument and the presentation.

2. **Listen.** In a 2014 interview on the CBC Radio 1 program *Q*, the musician and music producer Quincy Jones said the reason God has given humans one mouth and two ears is that listening is twice as important as speaking.[6] One of the biggest mistakes a debater can make is not to listen to what the other side has to say. In his *Rules*

of Conversation, William Penn wrote, "Some are so Foolish as to interrupt and anticipate those that speak, instead of hearing and thinking before they answer; which is uncivil as well as silly."[7] The best debaters are good listeners. They take notes as their opponents speak and immediately strategize in preparation for their rebuttal. When something your opponent says is unclear, seek clarification; ask questions. The *memory* canon of rhetoric applies here as you make use of your research to counter the opponent's arguments. If you listen well enough, the opposition will often provide you and your team with the ammunition you need to attack their arguments. And in the battle to win over the hearts and minds of the audience, it is probably a good strategy to at least appear as though you are listening. In that way you will not be faulted for being rude and or inconsiderate.

3. **Define your terms.** Be very clear about what you mean when you use key words and concepts. Your opponent may try to trip you up on your definitions. In fact, the entire debate may boil down to a dispute about the definition of one word. The famous twentieth-century historian Will Durant writes about Voltaire and the importance of defining one's terms: "If you wish to converse with me," said Voltaire, "define your terms." How many a debate would have been deflated into a paragraph if the disputants had dared to define their terms! The alpha and omega of logic, its heart and soul, is that every important term in serious discourse shall be subjected to the strictest scrutiny and definition. It is difficult, and it tests the mind ruthlessly, but once done it is half of any task.[8]

4. **Practice out loud.** The audience can usually tell when a speaker is uttering words out loud for the first time. Unless you have actually practised your argument out loud, your lack of confidence will almost always show. The audience will see that you are frightened and may be inclined to see your argument as weak before you've even had a chance to make it. Moreover, saying things out loud engages other communication centres in the brain (the ears, the mouth in addition to the eyes and other language and reasoning parts of the brain), and you are likely to pick up errors in logic as well as in spelling, grammar, and syntax.

5. **Practise your body language and gestures.** Again, the audience will notice if you are uncomfortable with certain movements or postures. Feeling physically comfortable conveys the idea to the audience that you are comfortable with the audience.

6. **Organization and timing.** As you practise out loud, time yourself to make sure that you can deliver the message in the time allowed. Remember the rule of three, and organize your evidence and your claims in order of importance to your overall argument.

7. **Anticipate your opponents' argument.** You and your team members should be very familiar with your opponent's argument before you've heard it and be able to respond immediately to their arguments. In fact, as we explain below, each of you should be able to summarize the opponents' arguments and anticipate the evidence they will present against your position. There should be no surprises.

During the Debate

1. **Summarize your opponent's argument.** Demonstrate that you have a clear and objective understanding of the other side's argument with an accurate summary of their argument. You may be able to identify

   a. those premises you both agree on

   b. those premises open to question and debate

   c. facts you can check and those that cannot be checked

   d. the difference between proven and unproven claims

   This will save time and focus the discussion on the real points of contention. The audience will thank you, and they may be won over by this show of grace, considerateness, and empathy.

2. **Give independent reasons that support and confirm your premises.** This proof, which comes in many forms, may include research, historical background, data from subject matter experts, or personal experience or observations.

3. **Agree where possible.** This strategy saves time and helps focus the debate on specific areas of disagreement. This show of empathy and reasonableness may even win over some audience members.

4. **Use your research.** If you've done the preparation, know your material, and have practised, you should be able to improvise and respond effectively to the opposition's counter-arguments.
5. **Offer constructive suggestions** that are in keeping with your argument. Remember that the objective of debating in political science is not victory, but the advancement of knowledge and civilized society.
6. **Speak slowly and clearly** to ensure that the audience can follow the logic of your argument and have time to absorb the message.
7. **Use non-verbal communication techniques** such as hand gestures, voice modulation, and eye contact to keep the audience engaged and sympathetic.

One final piece of advice that you may not always appreciate until the debate is over is to *enjoy the process and the challenge.* If you have done the preparation and moved beyond the initial jitters into the heat of the debate, you may actually find the act of debating quite enjoyable.

Rules of Engagement

It may be wise to remember that people with manners can always tell when someone lacks manners, and the audience may turn against a debater, not because of the quality of the arguments, but because he or she was rude. Here are a few basic rules of conduct to keep the proceedings orderly and civilized.

1. For the sake of fairness to each team, and for the audience's sake, adhere to the time allotted and respect the clock.
2. Allow one person to speak at a time.
3. Do not interrupt the members of the other team (or your own).
4. Speak politely to your opponents, avoid personal attacks, and be polite and respectful to your opponents and your own team members.
5. Instead of addressing the other debaters informally by using their first names, consider addressing them in a more respectful, formal way by using Mr or Ms and their surnames, or even "my honourable colleague."

So, to sum up, treat others the way you would like to be treated.

Debate Formats

This section, which is both for instructors and students, describes three types of debates: the formal debate, the rapid debate exercise, and the tag-team debate exercise. (Instructors can refer to the set-up instructions in organizing an in-class debate or a public event. Students may want to refer to these instructions in order to prepare for their own debate.)

There are many different styles of competitive debates, including Canadian, America, and British parliamentary debates, Mace debates, and Oxford-style debates. But for our purposes, we will stick to a few simple formats that are easily organized and can be performed in a small venue like a classroom or at a town hall meeting. In each type of debate format discussed below, a winner or winning side can be selected through a process common in the Oxford-style debate format. In the Oxford style, a topic is clearly defined and there is one team on each side of the issue. Before the debate begins, the audience is polled to determine which side of the issue they stand on, and when the debate is over the audience is polled again. The team with the majority of the audience on its side wins the debate. In every debate, the structure of the proceedings and the rules are there to make it easier for the teams to deliver their message and for the audience to listen to the message. Without a structure, rules of engagement, and/or a clock to keep track of time, a debate can easily degenerate into chaos or a waste of time.

Tools of the Trade

Regardless of which debate format is used, basic tools or equipment will be needed. Some items listed below are optional and may depend on which kind of debate is being held.

⊚   A seating plan and room arranged according to the type of debate
⊚   Chairs for the debating teams as well as the judges. Team members may want to sit as others stand to speak and do their work.
⊚   Three tables: one table for each team and one for the panel of judges
⊚   Pens and paper for writing notes—judges need to write notes, and team members may need to write notes to each other or may want to scribble notes as their opponents speak

- ◉ A stopwatch with which to time each team member's presentation
- ◉ A podium or two for the speakers
- ◉ A noisemaker to signal that the time is up
- ◉ Notes or cue cards as memory aids for the speakers

Formal Debate

After the thesis or the resolution has been chosen, a formal debate will involve the setting up of three groups:

1. The **Affirmative Team**: the group of two or three members supporting a thesis or a resolution
2. The **Opposing Team**: the group of two or three members opposing the resolution
3. The **Judges' Panel**: the group judging and critiquing the quality of the evidence and the presentation. The judging could also be done by your professor.

The debate organizers or instructor should make it clear what the rules of engagement are, how much time each person has to speak, and the room setup.

In preparation for the debate, each team will assign tasks to conduct research, gather evidence, and prepare logical arguments. Team members should strive to anticipate their opponents' arguments and to counter those arguments as well as preparing their own arguments. Once the team members have a clearer idea of the topic and how to argue their side of the resolution, they can plan the order of the member's presentations. Part of the preparation should include a live practice of the delivery. This should help with fine-tuning the argument, the delivery, and the timing.

Formal Debate Format

Affirmative Team—the first speaker for the Affirmative Team introduces their thesis and begins offering support for the resolution. (5–10 minutes)

Opposition Team—the first speaker for the Opposition Team introduces their thesis and begins offering support against the resolution. (5–10 minutes)

Affirmative Team—The second speaker on the Affirmative Team can present further arguments for the resolution and begin to indicate areas of conflict and address certain questions or points that may have been raised by the opposition. (5–10 minutes)

Opposition Team—Does the same as the second speaker on the Affirmative Team. (5–10 minutes)

Affirmative Team—The third team member offers the first rebuttal for the Affirmative Team. (3–5 minutes)

Opposition Team—The third team member offers the first rebuttal for the Opposition Team. (3–5 minutes)

Affirmative Team—The third team member offers the second rebuttal and closing argument for the Affirmative Team. (3–5 minutes)

Opposition Team—The third team member offers the second rebuttal and closing argument for the Opposition Team. (3–5 minutes)

(Estimated total time: 22 to 60 minutes)

Once the debate is over, the judges' panel can offer its critique. Audience members may want to offer their observations, contribute their comments on the topic, and ask questions. Team members may also wish to ask for comments from fellow students and reflect on their performance as well.

Tag-Team Debate

The tag-team debate format is helpful for getting students comfortable with argumentation in the classroom. It may be a good idea, before the debate begins, to instruct the students on what kinds of argumentation are acceptable, and to emphasize that everyone needs to be treated with courtesy.

Tag-Team Debate Format

Step 1—The first step involves dividing the classroom into opposing teams of three to five students. Each team is given one side of a controversial topic to argue, and they must prepare to debate a team with the opposite viewpoint. For example, one team may argue that public figures should have a right to privacy, while the other team will argue that the price of fame, fortune, and power is the right of the public to scrutinize the behaviour of public figures.

Step 2—The teacher or professor should allocate some time for research and preparation on the chosen topic and time to organize their argument. Research materials, such as books, articles, and editorials (preferably argumentative in nature), can also be made available to the students. Teams should also decide which team member speaks first in the debate.

Step 3—The final step is the actual debate. Two chairs are placed in the middle of the room: one chair for each starting speaker. A coin can be tossed to determine which side goes first. Only one speaker is allowed to speak at any one time. The starting team members should be given sufficient time to introduce their topic and make a point or two (3–5 minutes), but they should expect to be replaced by an alternate speaker from their team within a reasonable amount of time. Any team member who wishes to participate in the debate must tap their team member on the shoulder and replace them in the chair. At that point, the team member who has been tapped must stop talking immediately and cede the chair to his or her alternate. The alternate team member can continue speaking until he or she is tapped on the shoulder by another team member. If time allows, the same team members can participate in the debate more than once.

It may take one or two rounds for students to get comfortable with this exercise, but do not be surprised if they ask for a tag-team debate again. In fact, teachers should expect that other classmates or members of the audience will want to get in on the debate.

Rapid Debate

The rapid debate may be a good way to debate an issue when classroom time is of the essence. Split groups of four to six students into two debate teams; each team will argue one side of an issue or the other. For example: "Euthanasia should be legalized: agree or disagree."

Each group should be given enough time to prepare their arguments. In fact, this exercise works best when students have written an essay on one side of the issue before the debate.

Rapid-Debate Format

The table below indicates the sequence and the allotted time each side has to argue their case.

Debate Team Sequence	Allotted Time
1. Affirmative:	3 minutes
2. Opposition:	3 minutes
3. Affirmative Rebuttal:	3 minutes
4. Opposition Rebuttal:	3 minutes
5. Free-for-All:	4 minutes
6. Concluding Remarks, Opposition:	2 minutes
7. Concluding Remarks, Affirmative:	2 minutes
Total	20 minutes

Anyone who participates in these debate exercises will tell you that time goes by very quickly, and that in order to get your points across effectively, you need to be prepared and to have practised.

Conclusion

As the opening quotation suggests, we all win when the main purpose of the argument in a debate is to advance human understanding. Public speaking and debating require a combination of verbal and non-verbal communication techniques, some of which may take years to nurture and develop. Greek philosophers, for example, believed that only a virtuous person could become a great orator. Why? Because the great orators need to master the ability to balance *style* (the manner in which the argument is delivered) with *substance* (the factual evidence, the research methodology). It is no surprise, therefore, that training and practice have long been recommended for anyone wishing to enter professions such as politician, lawyer, or teacher, where public speaking or debating are one of the essential requirements of the job.

I hope that students come to see the importance of doing their research, of preparing their arguments and of practising out loud before any words are actually spoken in public. Students who are less comfortable with public speaking may want to prepare written statements and practise reading those statements out loud in a clear and expressive voice.

Another skill that students learn from this exercise is how to listen and to question when things are not clear. The other side will almost always say something that can be used in a counter-argument.

Review Exercises

1. In preparation for the debate, draw a mind map of your topic to help stimulate the creative juices and to ensure a thorough coverage of the issue.
2. Plan a debate by outlining the format, the time limits for each speaker, the seating, the scoring mechanism, and the rules of engagement.
3. Watch or read one of the speeches or the debates referred to above. Use the five canons of rhetoric to explain what makes the speaker or debater(s) effective. In view of the five canons, what would you improve?

Conclusion

There is no great share of probity necessary to support a monarchical or despotic government. The force of laws in one, and the prince's arm in the other, are sufficient to direct and maintain the whole. But in a popular state, one spring more is necessary, namely, virtue.

Montesquieu, Book III, *The Spirit of Laws*, 1748

What should the reader take away from this guide to research, writing, and debating? Our guide suggests that the social sciences, such as political science, can help you develop your ability to think critically and to communicate by showing you how to research, write, and argue. Research methods have been discussed at length, because without proper research—the uncovering of the factual evidence that supports the claim(s)—the argument will fail. With respect to essay writing, we've outlined the means of achieving good writing and of argumentation. The five canons of rhetoric were introduced as a means communicating and arguing effectively with a proper balance of style and substance. And we have discussed ways that you can practise your skills through debating exercises. But more important than all of this, we have argued that argumentation itself is a means of enhancing our quality of life.

In the spring of 2014, a radio journalist asked me whether, in light of the controversies surrounding the Rob Ford mayoralty, the Senate spending scandals, the voter suppression scandal from the 2011 general election, and the apparent disfunctionality of our parliamentary system of government, I believed the Canadian political system was "broken."

The question caught me off guard and I babbled something about Canadians have the ability to change governments peacefully and that if voters were more politically engaged we might get a better class of politician in government. However, this question did cause me to ponder the fragility of our democratic system of government and the nature of civil engagement.

There is a growing sense of urgency about the state of Canadian democracy. For many years political commentators such as Lawrence Martin of the *Globe and Mail*; Andrew Coyne of the CBC and *Maclean's* magazine; Rex Murphy of the CBC and the *National Post*; and even Preston Manning, political commentator and the former leader of the Reform Party of Canada, have expressed concern about an apparent decline in some of our democratic institutions.[1] They allude to many situations over several decades where successive Canadian governments, both Liberal and Conservative, have limited debate on matters important to Canadian society. One oft-cited example of stifling debate is the pushing through of so-called "omnibus bills" through our federal and provincial legislatures with the intent of avoiding conversations on topics that might be unpopular or controversial.

These and other pundits note that the behaviour of some federal politicians on the government side of the House lately who have shown contempt for Parliament by not giving clear answers to clear questions and for not providing information to Parliament when asked. Recall also that in April 2011, the Speaker of the House of Commons cited the Conservative government for contempt of Parliament because it had refused to provide Parliament with financial information about the purchase of fighter jets—the first in the history of the Commonwealth that that had happened. In fact, some MPs and ministers seem lately to be taking genuine pride in not answering the official Opposition's questions during question period.

Many have also pointed to a steady decline in the ability of our elected representatives to influence what goes on in government and to say what is on their minds without toeing the party line. Some federal cabinet ministers and MPs have even been compared to government sock puppets because of their apparent inability to speak without the aid of government talking points.[2]

And it's not just political commentators who lament this decline in our democratic institutions. More recently, Carol Goar, a columnist with the *Toronto Star*, reported that Canadians scientists had formed a collective called Scientists for the Right to Know because ". . . they could no longer watch helplessly as the government of Canada systematically stifled information on everything from climate change to drug safety." These scientists were compiling lists of public agencies that had been eliminated, knowledge programs that have been discarded, and the new restrictions that have been placed on public officials. In the opinion of their president, Margit Eichler, "Canadians are being made ignorant about our country and ourselves. . . . Good policies must be based on solid evidence. Democracy requires an informed electorate."[3]

Indeed to many Canadians, Parliament itself has forgotten its purpose. And this has led to the cynical and substantiated view that our elected representatives have become little more than a rubber stamp for their government bosses. Perhaps as a result of this powerlessness on the part of the people we elected to govern on our behalf, a large proportion of Canadian citizens have lost faith in the ability of our democratic institutions to do what is necessary for the people. Being a "citizen" is no longer fashionable. The current fashion in some political parties is to see a citizen or voter as a shopper for political brands and political products. Citizens no longer need to be engaged in the political process.[4] The citizens and the politicians have forgotten that it is these institutions that help large and complex societies to manage power, to change our governments regularly, and to resolve our conflicts peacefully. These very institutions, when they function well, as they have in Canada since 1848 with the introduction of responsible government to our political system, have protected us from descending into the kind of political chaos we have seen recently in countries like Syria, Zimbabwe, and Ukraine.

What, then, are we to make of this apparent decline in decorum and faith in our democratic institutions and why does it matter? The pattern that emerges from much of our recent politics is that somehow we have forgotten the value of a good argument. Konrad Yakabuski of the *Globe and Mail* writes:

Intuition, ideas and passion used to matter in politics. Now, data analytics aims to turn all politicians into robots, programmed to deliver a script that has been scientifically tested . . . .

Politics is no longer about the art of persuasion or about having an honest debate about what's best for your country, province or city. It's about microtargeting individuals who've already demonstrated on their Facebook posts or responses to telephone surveys that they are suggestible. Voters are data points to be manipulated, not citizens to be cultivated.[5]

Rather than an argument being appreciated as an opportunity to learn from each other and to advance the cause of knowledge and of civilization, an argument is now mostly seen as something to be tolerated at best and, at worst, despised and eradicated like some kind of pestilence or noxious weed.

What is missing in our politics is an appreciation of why good argumentation matters to the democratic system of government. As pointed out in Chapter 5, the Greeks believed that only the most virtuous could achieve great oratory because the virtuous person possessed the kind moral excellence and proper balance of human characteristics that could lead to better ideas and inspiration that could lead to greatness. For Montesquieu, who wrote extensively in the 1700s on the nature of politics and the benefits of democracy, virtue was the willingness of the individual to put the community ahead of the individual. And for him, the fundamental principle of democracy was political virtue. Montesquieu based his theory of democracy on his observations of political history and his practice of law.

Virtue in a republic is a most simple thing: it is a love of the republic; it is a sensation, and not a consequence of acquired knowledge: a sensation that may be felt by the meanest as well as by the highest person in the state. When the common people adopt good maxims, they adhere to them more steadily than those whom we call gentlemen. It is very rarely that corruption commences with the former: nay, they frequently derive from their imperfect light a stronger attachment to the established laws and customs.[6]

One way to develop the virtuous behaviour that many philosophers speak of is by learning and practising critical thinking. As a reminder of what we have discussed in the previous chapters, here are a few essay-writing and debating guidelines to live by:

- *State your purpose.* What you are arguing should not be mysterious. The *thesis* names the topic of your argument, essay or debate, and states its main purpose.
- *The introduction is the most important part of any debate speech or essay* because it is an agreement or contract between you and the listener or reader. Everything that is written or said after the introduction will be compared to your introduction. Do not hesitate to rewrite the introduction after you have finished writing the essay or speech. It is time well-spent.
- *Good writing and argumentation have a rhythm.* The number three is important because it indicates that there is a pattern; therefore, in order to prove there is a pattern, include three or more pieces of evidence (statistics, historical examples, experts, etc.) in your essay.
- Each piece of *evidence must be specific and relevant* to the thesis in every way.
- Supporting *facts must be accurate and their source must be given*; it is far preferable to over-report your references than under-reporting them.
- *Show how ideas and evidence are connected.*
- *Check each sentence for spelling, proper structure (syntax), grammar, and punctuation.*
- *Consider the flip side of the coin.* Your opponents may have a point or a perspective worth exploring. If not, you need to demonstrate why.
- The *conclusion must be an effective restatement of the essay's main argument* and must leave no doubt in the listener's or reader's mind about your position. The message should be repeated one last time to set a pattern that people remember.
- Finally, remember that factual evidence is certainly important for appealing to people's minds and to winning the argument, but that style is what appeals to their hearts.

It may be time for Canadian citizens to rediscover what it means to live in a democracy and to be reminded that while citizenship bestows rights, privileges, and entitlement, it also imposes obligations. One of these obligations—as important as voting, paying taxes, obeying the law, and fighting for one's country while at war—is that we hold the politicians and our governmental institutions to account and that corruption and tyranny need to be held in check at all times. Some students think I am joking when I tell them that the main reason I teach Canadian politics is to make sure that they don't screw things up for me and my family. While some students find the statement humorous, the state of our democracy is not a laughing matter: How do we prevent politicians from hurting our society and hurting future generations? We share are responsibility to each other to know the facts when we vote. I have argued here that we do this by beginning the lifelong process of learning about what makes an argument good and how to argue effectively among ourselves in a manner that is, as the Greeks and Montesquieu said, virtuous. That is the obligation we take on when we agree to live in a democracy. We renew the social contract every time we vote. And in this way, we ensure that our politicians offer good arguments in justification for their actions. Good arguments do matter, and it would be a good thing for more citizens to believe that to argue well is to live well.

Glossary

The following definitions, unless otherwise indicated, were either taken from or based upon the *Canadian Oxford Dictionary*.

affirmative assertion that a thing is so

annotated bibliography a list of works consulted with a brief description of or explanatory note about each one

argument (1) an exchange of views; (2) a reason advanced; a reasoning process; (3) summary of the subject matter or line of reasoning in a particular essay, article, book, or documentary

argumentation methodical reasoning designed to prove, make clear, or advance a point of view

artificial grassroots organization an organization which is created by an association or company with a vested interest in government policy on, for example, manufactured products, drugs, health products, the media, real-estate development, agricultural products, and which attempts to influence such government policy by appearing to be a genuine grassroots organization

barroom guess a groundless opinion and prediction that is not based on fact

bibliography a list of books referred to in a scholarly work

claim a statement or assertion that something is true or false

classification a systematic distribution of information or material into categories

con against (in reference to a proposition)

concluding (closing) sentence a sentence that summarizes and ties all of the ideas contained in the paragraph together

conclusion an inference from given premises or a judgment reached by reason

criterion validity a test or measure can be valid if it compares favourably with other tests and measures already known to be valid

critical thinking the systematic evaluation or formulation of belief statements by rational standards

debate a discussion about a proposal or a claim

debatable questionable or subject to dispute

deductive reasoning the inferring of particular instances from a general law

definition a statement of the meaning of words or the nature of a thing

dependent variable the phenomenon one is trying to explain

descriptive writing writing that serves as a description or seeks to describe without expressing judgment or feeling

dogma a belief or set of beliefs that is held by an authority or group and which others are expected to accept without argument (an arrogant declaration of opinion)

educated guess an opinion or prediction based on factual evidence

empirical data information collected through the senses

empirical based or acting on observation or experimentation rather than theory

essay a written composition on any subject

epistemology the study of knowledge or the science of science

evidence the available facts, circumstances, observations, and so on that support a belief or proposition

experimental validity in scientific research, the extent to which a conclusion is valid because of the soundness and ethics of the research design

expert a person trained by experience

explicit knowledge theoretical understanding

expository writing writing intended to explain or describe something in detail

extrinsic proof proof that is not invented by the person making the argument, but is used in support of the thesis

face validity the idea that a test or experiment has validity when it *looks* as if it will measure what is says it will measure

fact something that can be measured or verified

factoid an assumption or speculation that is reported or repeated so often that it becomes accepted as fact

fallacy (1) an argument that is not logical; (2) an argument that is unsound by virtue of its rhetoric or logic

generalization a proposition or general notion obtained by inference from limited or inadequate cases

ghost writer a person who wrote on behalf of the person who is credited as the author of a work

hypothesis an assumption that needs to be tested against relevant evidence

implicit knowledge practical skills

independent variable the factor that affects the dependent variable

induction the inference of a particular law from particular instances

inductive reasoning the inferring a particular law from specific instances

inference the forming of a conclusion from premises

informed opinion a belief formed on the basis of fact

intervening variable a factor that can influence both the dependent and independent variables

intrinsic proof a proof used in the argument that is inherent in the object or subject, such as definitions, named parts, species or characteristics, comparisons, and so on

introduction the explanatory section at the beginning of a speech, documentary, essay or book

intuition the power of understanding situations or people's feelings immediately, without the need for conscious reasoning or study

knowledge a theoretical and practical understanding of a subject

logic the science of reasoning, proof, thinking, and inference

mind map a diagram or drawing representing and organizing ideas, connections, images, and words around a single concept

model a theoretical and simplified (often visual) representations or description of reality

narrative writing a written account of connected events in the order in which they happened

natural law an unchanging scientific or moral principle common to the universe or to all people

news information about important or interesting recent events, especially when published or broadcast

opinion a belief or assessment based on grounds short of proof; a view held as probable

oratory the art or practice of formal speaking in public. Also known as **public speaking**

paradigm (1) an example of something or a pattern of phenomena that are observed in society and can be used to identify a trend; (2) a way of looking at the world; (3) a way of looking at a phenomenon in order to explain it

paragraph a distinct passage of text, considering the subject from one particular point of view

peer review a process by which written work is reviewed, evaluated, and critiqued by professional peers before being published

perception the faculty of perceiving or the intuitive recognition of a truth

perspective the apparent relation between visible objects as to position or distance; point of view or a way of regarding a matter

plagiarism taking another person's words, ideas, invention, research, or property, and passing it off as one's own

politics a human activity for managing power and conflict

premise a statement or reason given in support of a conclusion

proposition a statement of claim that is subject to proof or disproof

predictive validity the extent to which a test or measure can be relied upon to predict outcomes for certain populations and in specific situations

premise a statement or proposition put forth in support of a conclusion; a previous statement from which another statement is inferred

primary sources the original observations, artifacts, research findings, or documents that have not been digested, summarized, classified, compared or analyzed in any way

pro for or in favour (in reference to a proposition)

propaganda an organized program of publicity, selected information, or even distortions of the truth, used to propagate a doctrine, practice, policy

proposition a statement of claim that is subject to proof or disproof

public speaking *see* **oratory**

qualitative not quantitative, verifiable, or subject to measurement

quantitative able to be measured and verified

refutation that part of the argument where the speaker anticipates or refutes opposing points of view

reliable dependable and consistent in character and in quality

resource anything that can be used to achieve an end, such as money, people, property, and raw material

research the systematic investigation into and study of materials, sources, etc. in order to establish facts and reach new conclusions

research methodology a systematic and defined set of procedures used in conducting research and common to all the sciences

rhetoric the art of effective or persuasive speaking or writing

selection bias the existence on the part of persons conducting research of prejudices or preconceived notions that may damage the objectivity of the research and the evidence from that research

science a branch of knowledge based on objective principles involving the systematized observation of and experimentation with phenomena

scientific according to the rules laid down in exact science for performing observations and testing the soundness of conclusions

secondary source product of a writer, journalist and scientist, who has used primary sources to report or comment on a phenomenon, trend, or event

sophistry use of intentionally deceptive or specious arguments or reasoning

statistic statistical fact or item

statistics the science of collecting and analyzing numerical data, especially in large quantities, and usually inferring proportions in a whole from proportions in a representative sample

subject matter expert (SME) a person or institution that is recognized as an objective and reliable source of information and opinion on a particular subject

supporting sentence a sentence designed to explain, expand upon, or support the topic sentence. A supporting sentence can be a fact, a definition, an example, or a quotation that illustrates the point

suppression actions by the organs of the state to manipulate the truth and discourage open discussion

taxonomy a type of classification that organizes information in a subject area and makes connections between the data and the thesis

theory an explanation, system of ideas, or mental conception about something.

thesis a proposition (or claim) to be maintained or proved

topic sentence a general statement that highlights and summarizes the main idea of that paragraph

transition word a commonly used word or phrase that establish a link between one idea and the next, between sentences, and between one paragraph and the next

typology a classification of human characteristics or behaviour according to type

understand (1) (empirical) perceive the significance, explanation, or cause of something through reasoning and comprehension; (2) (intuitive) have a sympathetic awareness of the character or the nature of something

valid sound, well-founded, and defensible

values a belief in what is important, valuable, or ethical or the principles or moral standards of a person or society

variable a factor that can cause quantitative and qualitative changes

warrant permission, authorization, or licence to make an inference and accept the claim

Endnotes

Preface

1. Canadian Broadcasting Corporation, "The Great Human Odyssey," *The Nature of Things*, 12 February 2015.
2. Samara Canada, *Lightweights? Political Participation beyond the Ballot Box*, accessed 26 March 2015, http://www.samaracanada.com/research/active-citizenship/lightweights
3. Alex Preston, "The War against Humanities at Britain's Universities," *The Guardian*, 29 March 2015. http://www.theguardian.com/education/2015/mar/29/war-against-humanities-at-britains-universities.
4. "Is Politics Broken?" *CBC Asks*, March 2015, http://www.cbc.ca/news/politics/cbc-asks-is-politics-broken-team-no-weighs-in-1.3003046.

Introduction

1. Thomas Hobbes, *Of Man, Being the First Part of Leviathan*, Chapter XIII, Of the Natural Condition of Mankind as Concerning Their Felicity and Misery.
2. Definitions, unless otherwise indicated, are from the *Canadian Oxford Dictionary*, Thumb Index Edition (Don Mills, ON: Oxford University Press, 1998).
3. Excerpt from Joseph Heath, *Enlightenment 2.0: Restoring Sanity to Our Politics, Our Economy, and Our Lives* (Toronto: HarperCollins, 2014), p. 2. Published by HarperCollins Ltd. All rights reserved.
4. Ibid., pp. 58–59.
5. Social scaffolding is a concept introduced in the 1950s by the cognitive psychologist Jerome Bruner to describe how children acquire language, but it has since developed into a concept used to explain how humans acquire knowledge.
6. Heath, *Enlightenment*, p. 185.
7. Michael Ignatieff, *The Lesser Evil: Political Ethics in an Age of Terror,* (Princeton: Princeton University Press, 2005), pp. 169–170.

8. R. Paul and L. Elder, *Critical Thinking: Concepts and Tools* (Dillon Beach, CA: Foundation for Critical Thinking, 2007). Discussed and quoted in Thomas Arcaro and Rosemary Haskell, *Understanding the Global Experience: Becoming a Responsible World Citizen* (Boston: Allyn & Bacon, 2010), p. 150.
9. Many of the *National Post* articles listed here speak to the lack of civility and of the attempts by some members of Parliament, notably the Conservative MP Michael Chong, to reform parliamentary procedures to encourage rational debate and civility. http://fullcomment.nationalpost.com/tag/question-period/.
10. Lewis Vaughn and Chris MacDonald, *The Power of Critical Thinking*, 3rd edn, (Don Mills, ON: Oxford University Press, 2013), p. 3.
11. David Hume, *Enquiries Concerning Human Understanding and Concerning the Principles of Morals*, 3rd edn (Oxford: Clarendon Press, 1975), p. 14.
12. Stanford University, *Aristotle's Political Theory*, 2011, http://plato.stanford.edu/entries/aristotle-politics/; Kenneth Minogue, *Politics: A Very Short Introduction* (London: Oxford University Press, 1995); quotation from Paul Valéry taken from http://www.quotationspage.com/quote/163.html; quotation from Ambrose Bierce taken from http://en.wikiquote.org/wiki/Ambrose_Bierce.
13. Lao Tzu, *Tao Te Ching*, http://www.sacred-texts.com/tao/salt/salt08.htm.
14. Allan Bloom, trans., *The Republic of Plato* (New York: Basic Books, 1968).
15. Aristotle: "Politics," in Ernest Barker ed. and trans., *The Politics of Aristotle* (New York, Oxford University Press, 1976).
16. Max Weber: *Politics as a Vocation,* http://anthropos-lab.net/wp/wp-content/

uploads/2011/12/Weber-Politics-as-a-Vocation.pdf.

17. A good discussion of some of David Easton's important writings on politics can be found at http://www.mmisi.org/pr/01_01/miller.pdf.

Chapter 1

1. David Hume, *Essays, Moral, Political, and Literary*, 1742, section I.III.1 and I.III.8 http://www.econlib.org/library/LFBooks/Hume/hmMPL3.html.

2. Ted Benton, *Philosophical Foundations of the Three Sociologies* (London: Routledge & Kegan Paul, 1977), p. 83.

3. Bertrand Russell, *The Scientific Outlook* (Electronic Edition, Gutenberg, 1954).

4. Russell, *The Problems of Philosophy* (Electronic Edition, Gutenberg, 1912).

5. Quotations from Daniel J. Boorstin taken from http://www.goodreads.com/author/quotes/10378.Daniel_J_Boorstin; quotations from Ellison, Chesterton, and Solzhenitsyn taken from http://en.wikiquote.org/.

Chapter 2

1. List of offences obtained from Daily Source, *Current Problems in the Media*, http://www.dailysource.org/about/problems#U9pfybHQrZ8.

2. Rosanna Tamburri, "Long-form Census Remains Hot Topic for Canadian Researchers," 3 June 2012, http://www.universityaffairs.ca/news/news-article/long-form-census-remains-hot-topic-for-canadian-researchers/. Used with permission from Rosanna Tamburri University Affairs, June 4, 2012.

3. Daily Source, *Current Problems in the Media*, http://www.dailysource.org/about/problems#U9pfybHQrZ8.

4. Robert E. Babe and Jessica Potter, "Media Ownership," *The Canadian Encyclopedia*, 4 March 2015, http://www.thecanadianencyclopedia.ca/en/article/media-ownership/.

5. Dillan Theckedath and Terrence J. Thomas, *Media Ownership and Convergence in Canada*, Industry, Infrastructure and Resources Division, Library of Parliament, 10 April 2012, p. 3, http://www.parl.gc.ca/content/lop/researchpublications/2012-17-e.pdf.

6. Neil Henry, quoted in "Academe and the Decline of News Media," *The Chronicle of Higher Education*, 5 November 2009, http://chronicle.com/article/Academethe-Decline-of/49120/.

7. Sharon Beder, "Public Relations' Role in Manufacturing Artificial Grass Roots Coalitions," *Public Relations Quarterly* 43(2), Summer 98, pp. 21–23.

8. Alain de Botton, *The News: A User's Manual*, Toronto: McClelland Stewart, 2014, p. 243. Excerpt(s) from *The News: A User's Manual* by Alain De Botton, copyright © 2014 by Alain De Botton. Used by permission of Pantheon Books, an imprint of the Knopf Doubleday Publishing Group, a division of Penguin Random House LLC. All rights reserved.

9. Ibid. pp. 244–245.

10. Wikipedia.org, editing criteria, http://en.wikipedia.org/wiki/Wikipedia:Introduction.

11. De Botton, *The News*, p. 242.

12. For more on statistics and their uses, go to http://www.socialresearchmethods.net/kb/statdesc.php.

13. Unesco.org, Ethical Guidelines for International Comparative Politics (accessed 25 April 2015) http://www.unesco.org/most/ethical.htm.

14. Seneca Libraries, Seneca College of Applied Arts and Technology, North York, 2013.

15. Ibid.

16. Ibid., Library Research Worksheet, adapted from a user form developed by Seneca Libraries.

Chapter 3

1. Rex Murphy, "Universities have become factories for reinforcing opinion," *National Post*, 12 April 2014, http://news.nationalpost.com/full-comment/rex-murphy-on-ayaan-hirsi-ali-universities-have-become-factories-for-reinforcing-opinion.

2. Jim Sanford, "That Strong Recovery? It Was Just a Myth," *Globe and Mail,* 11 August 2014. Used by permission of Jim Stanford.
3. Based on grammar.ccc.commnet.edu, The Principles of Organization, http://grammar.ccc.commnet.edu/grammar/composition/organization.htm.
4. Based on University of Ottawa's Student Academic Services resources, http://sass.uottawa.ca/sites/sass.uottawa.ca/files/transition-words_2.pdf.
5. Canadian Institutes of Health Research, Natural Sciences and Engineering Research Council of Canada, Social Sciences and Humanities Research Council of Canada, *Tri-Council Policy Statement: Ethical Conduct for Research Involving Humans,* December 2010 http://www.pre.ethics.gc.ca/pdf/eng/tcps2/TCPS_2_FINAL_Web.pdf.
6. Christin Rushowy, "TDSB's Chris Spence Resigns Amid Growing Plagiarism Scandal," *Toronto Star,* 1 October, 2013. http://www.thestar.com/news/gta/2013/01/10/tdsbs_chris_spence_resigns_amid_growing_plagiarism_scandal.html.

Chapter 4

1. John Poulakos, definition of Sophists quoted in grammar.about.com, *Encyclopedia of Rhetoric,* accessed 15 August 2014, http://grammar.about.com/od/rs/g/Sophiststerm.htm.
2. National Council for Excellence in Critical Thinking, Founding Principles, accessed 1 August 2014, http://www.criticalthinking.org/pages/the-national-council-for-excellence-in-critical-thinking/406.
3. Theory of argumentation and sample arguments based on Vaughn and MacDonald, *The Power of Critical Thinking,* 3rd Edition, Oxford University Press, Toronto, 2013, p. 68–78.
4. Based on an example in David Zarefsky, *Argumentation: The Study of Effective*

Reasoning, 2nd edn (Chantilly, VA: The Great Courses, 2005), pp. 28–30.
5. Alison Bethel McKenzie, *Use with Care: A Reporter's Glossary of Loaded Language in the Israeli–Palestinian Conflict* (Vienna: International Press Institute, ethicaljournalismnetwork.org), http://ethicaljournalismnetwork.org/en/contents/use-with-care-a-reporter-s-glossary-of-loaded-language-in-the-israeli-palestinian-conflict.
6. Adapted from Kay Lawson, *The Human Polity: A Comparative Introduction to Political Science* (New York: Wadsworth, 2002).
7. Vaughn and MacDonald, *The Power of Critical Thinking,* pp. 377–89.
8. For interest's sake, have a look at http://en.wikipedia.org/wiki/List_of_fallacies#Formal_fallacies.
9. Classification of fallacies based on Vaughn and MacDonald, *The Power of Critical Thinking,* pp. 391–94.

Chapter 5

1. "Aristotle's Rhetoric, Three Means of Persuasion," in *Stanford Encyclopedia of Philosophy* (Stanford Education, 2010), Section 5, accessed December 12, 2014. http://plato.stanford.edu/entries/aristotle-rhetoric/#4.3.
2. Ibid., "The Purpose of Rhetoric," Section 4.
3. The discussion of canons of rhetoric is based on http://rhetoric.byu.edu/canons/Canons.htm.
4. Quoted from Toastmasters International http://www.toastmasters.org/MainMenuCategories/FreeResources/NeedHelpGivingaSpeech/TipsTechniques/10TipsforPublicSpeaking.aspx.
5. Based on an interview with Micheal Vonn (policy director of the BC Civil Liberties Association), "An Advocate's Top Five Misconceptions about Free Speech," CBC, *The 180,* 18 January 2015, http://www.cbc.ca/radio/the180/carbon-taxes-freedom-of-speech-zero-tuition-1.2900918/an-advocate-

s-top-five-misconceptions-about-free-speech-1.2901045.

6. Quincy Jones, interviewed by Jian Ghomeshi, CBC Radio, *Q*, http://www.cbc.ca/q/blog/2014/05/20/quincy-jones/.

7. William Penn, Rule #130, Fruits of Solitude. Part I, *Rules of Conversation*, The Harvard Classics, 1909–14, http://www.bartleby.com/1/3/.

8. Voltaire discussed in Will Durant, *The Story of Philosophy* (New York: Pocket Books, 1991).

Conclusion

1. Here is a small sample of articles, essays, and videos from the political pundits mentioned here:

   a. Lawrence Martin, *Is This Still a Democracy? You Be the Judge*, http://www.ipolitics.ca/2012/04/27/lawrence-martin-is-this-still-a-democracy-you-be-the-judge/.

   b. Josh Wingrove, "Preston Manning Criticizes Harper's Electoral Reform," http://www.theglobeandmail.com/news/politics/preston-manning-criticizes-harpers-electoral-reform-efforts/article17185699/#dashboard/follows/.

   c. Andrew Coyne, *The Reform Acts Lessons*. http://fullcomment.nationalpost.com/2014/09/12/andrew-coyne-on-the-reform-acts-lesson-party-leaders-have-made-canadian-democracy-unreformable/.

   d. Rex Murphy, Tom Mulcair, Paul Calandra, and the Speaker, http://www.cbc.ca/player/News/TV+Shows/The+National/Politics/ID/2531313587/.

2. On the decline of debate in the House of Commons, see http://www.cbc.ca/player/News/TV+Shows/The+National/Politics/ID/2531375570/.

3. Carol Goar, "Scientists Fight to Roll Back the Darkness," *Toronto Star*, 3 October 2014, p. A17.

4. Susan Delacourt, *Shopping for Votes: How Politicians Choose Us and We Choose Them* (Vancouver: Douglas and McIntyre, 2013).

5. Konrad Yakabuski, "The Lost Art of Political Persuasion," *Globe and Mail*, 25 April 2015, p. F2.

6. Montesquieu, *The Spirit of Laws*, Book V, 1748.

Index